Knowing Lecrae's unique story and gifts, this book has been a long time coming and is essential to not only those interested in his music and hip-hop, but also those wanting to better understand the intersection between faith and culture and what it looks like to be in the world but not of it.

Matt Chandler, lead pastor of The Village Church, president of the Acts 29, author of *The Mingling of Souls*

Honest. Rare. Freeing. Lecrae is one of the most talented people I know. His story will leave you inspired and challenged. *Unashamed* reminds us just how powerful the gospel is. Jesus turns our scars into our stories. This is a story you will want to read!

Louie Giglio, Passion City Church / Passion Conferences, author of *The Comeback*

It's a rare privilege to see a prophetic story unfold before your very eyes. When it does, you pay attention. Lecrae's *Unashamed* gives us the raw account of a rare leader, stirred by the heart of God to shape culture by creating it.

Gabe Lyons, Q, author of *Good Faith*

Lecrae's story is as real as it gets. The rawness, pain, and brutal honesty make it a tremendously gripping read. But the sheer beauty of his journey to redemption makes it something you'll want to share with others, and I certainly hope you will. This book will change lives.

Eric Metaxas, *New York Times* best-selling author of *Bonhoeffer and Miracles*

Lecrae has never fit in any boxes, and in this book he once again breaks the mold to create an identity all his own—the hip-hop artist as worldview thinker. The book starts by relating the emotionally turbulent, completely absorbing story of his life, and ends by presenting his innovative thoughts on a Christian worldview approach to hip-hop. Lecrae continues to be a delightfully unpredictable anomaly.

Nancy Pearcey, author of *Total Truth* and *Finding Truth*

If you love beautiful music, powerful stories, or the Lord Jesus Christ, you will not be able to put this book down. Lecrae doesn't hold back in *Unashamed*; there is no "Christian-ese" or posturing in this memoir. Instead, he takes the reader through his grace-filled journey from abandonment to community, from brokenness to wholeness, from a life lost in the world to one found in the arms of God. This must-read book is for hip-hop heads and believers, artists and seekers, and anyone who wants to know more about one of the most compelling artists of our time. I expect that millions of people will read this book, discover more about Lecrae, and be inspired to walk with Jesus themselves, unashamed.

Joshua DuBois, spiritual advisor to President Obama, author of *The President's Devotional*, founder of Values Partnerships

This is an artistic coming-of-age story with all the brokenness and beauty of our American reality and our Christian hope. It's not just the story of how a boy became a man, or how a lost soul found faith, but how an artist found his voice. There's so much here for those who care about the intersection of deep faith with great art. Lecrae is showing the rest of us how it is done.

Andy Crouch, executive editor, *Christianity Today*,
author of *Culture Making: Recovering Our Creative Calling*

From extreme humble beginnings to what many would describe as a dream platform, Lecrae puts his journey in perspective. He recognizes all too well the identity crisis and this generation's need to be unashamed of the gospel. I recommend this book for whomever is interested in seeing how God is authoring the journey of a fatherless generation in need of the navigator.

Eric Mason, lead pastor, Epiphany Fellowship,
author of *Unleashed*

UN–
ASHAMED
LECRAE

WITH JONATHAN MERRITT

UN–
ASHAMED
LECRAE

WITH JONATHAN MERRITT

B&H
PUBLISHING GROUP
NASHVILLE, TENNESSEE

978-1-4336-8912-3

Published by B&H Publishing Group
Nashville, Tennessee

Dewey Decimal Classification: B
Subject Heading: MOORE, LECRAE \ RAP
MUSICIANS—BIOGRAPHY \ CHRISTIAN LIFE

Published in association with Yates & Yates,
www.yates2.com.

1 2 3 4 5 6 • 21 20 19 18 17 16

FOR BIG MOMMA

I AM THE MAN I AM TODAY BECAUSE OF
THE SEEDS YOU SOWED IN MY LIFE.

CONTENTS

O -
RED CARPET
TREATMENT

———

I tried my best to fit in
Looking for a suit to fit in
Standing outside of your prison
Trying to find ways I could get in
Now I realize that I'm free
And I realize that I'm me
And I found out that I'm not alone
Cause' there's plenty people like me
That's right there's plenty people like me
All love me, despite me
And all unashamed and all unafraid to speak out for what we
might see
. . . All outsiders like me.

Lecrae | "Outsiders" | *Anomaly*

———

The paparazzi's cameras were flashing, but their lenses were all pointed at someone else.

I was at the Staples Center in Los Angeles, California, attending the 2015 Grammy Awards ceremony. I'd been nominated for "Best Rap Performance" and was competing against the likes of Eminem, Drake, and Kendrick Lamar. I had already won two Grammys, but this was different.

Many people don't know that not all Grammy Awards are created equal. An unspoken hierarchy exists in many circles, and some categories are more respected than others. Within the music world, if you tell someone you won a Grammy, the first follow-up question is "Which category?" Though I'm grateful for my wins for "Best Gospel Album" and "Best Contemporary Christian Music Performance," as you might guess, some consider those closer to the bottom of the list than the top. But this nomination for "Best Rap Performance" had a different kind of significance. It told the world that an alternative voice with an alternative message was being considered among the biggest artists of our time. It said that the industry had finally recognized a new way of making hip-hop.

That's why I was so mad at myself when I arrived late to the red carpet after promising I'd get there early. It was a rookie mistake. The biggest stars show up just before show time, so all the younger and lesser-known artists know to arrive early to avoid competing with Katy Perry for interviews. Even a few minutes can make a difference between landing a blurb in *Rolling Stone* and hearing crickets.

When I stepped out of the car, I thought to myself, *You are at the Grammys, man.* I tried to just be in the moment and not look at the stands where fans were sitting and pointing and criticizing every fold and shade of fabric. There I was, taking a coveted walk and rubbing shoulders with John Legend, Kanye West, Chris Brown, and Meghan Trainor. It was difficult to believe that after all of the writing and rapping and refining and recording and touring and promoting and praying, I stood there.

But as it turned out, walking the red carpet at the 2015 Grammys was a more complicated affair than I had imagined. People kept passing on interviews, and some were painfully attempting to not even make eye contact with me.

"Hey, that reporter looks like they are trying to get my attention," I thought. "Wait . . . no . . . they are waving at Questlove."

When I reached the end of the carpet—you know, the place where artists stand in front of the Grammys backdrop and a crowd of photographers takes their picture—a security guard lowered his hand and asked me to wait. He waved Iggy Azalea around me. She smiled, and the cameras went crazy. When she finished, I started to proceed but the security guard stopped me again. He waved Rick Ross through.

This happened so many times I lost count. Wiz Khalifa and then Taylor Swift and then Keith Urban and then Ziggy Marley. Somewhere in the process my wife threw up her hands and left me to go sit down. For forty-five minutes I waited until the security guard finally raised his arm and waved me through.

I walked in front of the backdrop in my crisp tuxedo and shiny shoes, standing tall and proud as a nominee in a respected category. I gave them the best smile I had. And . . . almost every journalist lowered their camera. Maybe

03

five of the forty photographers took my picture, and I'm pretty sure those were snapped out of pity.

Some people say the red carpet is the best litmus test for how famous you are or how famous you're not. For how accepted you are or aren't. If this is true, the message was clear: I am not one of "them."

I started to get that feeling earlier in the day at Jay Z and Beyonce's "Roc Nation" party on a lawn tucked behind a Beverly Hills mansion. I'm kind of a people-watcher and also an introvert, so I made up my mind before arriving that I was going to sink back and mind my business.

The event was a whirlwind of hype and hustle. The smell of cigars and fancy French perfume filled the air while bartenders poured bottle after bottle of "Ace of Spades" champagne. Everyone was draped in borrowed jewelry and clothes made by designers that most people can't pronounce. Italian shoes, thousand-dollar jeans, tiny but noticeable logos on pockets and lapels. (Fashion is something of an art for musicians, so everyone tries to strike a balance between the brand being obvious, but downplayed.)

It quickly became clear that there were two classes of people. In the center of the yard was the first class: epic stars—Jay Z and Kanye and Nicki Minaj and Rihanna. They were sitting on couches under a gazebo with security surrounding them.

And around the gazebo was the second class: everyone else. These were people from the famous, to the famous-ish, to the hope-to-be famous. They were all talented and successful, but not part of the pantheon who exist in the stratosphere of super-celebrities. Many of them were

04

hovering around the couches, pretending not to be mesmerized and hoping to get noticed.

After about twenty minutes of people watching, I snapped out of my daze and realized something: nobody had initiated a conversation with me. No one, that is, except for record executives who thought I could make them some money. I stood on the outside, barely part of the second group. While everyone else was congregating and high-fiving, I was just taking up space.

People who've only seen me perform might assume that I'm confident and that being ignored wouldn't bother me—but it does. There was actually a fight inside of me. Sure, I was turned off by the way it all felt a little like high school, with everyone trying to be one of the cool kids or at least friends with the cool kids. The only difference is that this is all happening with adults who know better. Everyone goes to the bathroom and gets nervous and has family drama. Everyone is no more or less human than anyone else. So the whole thing felt a little trivial and silly.

And yet, another part of me wanted to be there. To be a part of the in-crowd. To be liked and respected and noticed. Who doesn't want to be accepted? But I'm not— at least not in the same way.

You might assume I was an outsider because I was the "new kid" and people just didn't know who I was. But as record executives started introducing me to others, I discovered this was not true.

"I want you to meet Lecrae," the record executive would often say. "He's a *Christian* rapper."

"I know who you are," they would respond with a patronizing smile. "I'm familiar with your music."

05

The awkwardness would grow, and I could almost hear their thoughts: *Can I cuss around him? Is he about to preach at me, or judge me if I drink this whole bottle of Cristal and stumble out of here?* Maybe they don't know if they can be fully themselves around me. Or perhaps they don't think they would like the content of my music or the assumptions behind my music or the worldview I hold. Regardless, they don't want to know more. From that point on, it felt awkward. It was like I was marked.

This isn't the first time I've felt shunned because of people's preconceptions. A few years ago, for example, I was invited to attend a Sacramento Kings basketball team practice. I brought a bunch of my newly released *Church Clothes* mixtapes to give to anyone who was interested. When I was introduced, the person said, "Hey, y'all. We've got a Gospel rapper here who has some music if you want it."

No one picked up an album.

After getting into a conversation with one of the players, I asked him if he wanted some music. "Nah, man," he said, "I don't do Gospel rap. I don't want all those Bible verses and preaching." I tried to tell him my album wasn't like that—it addressed issues like fatherlessness and insecurity, things that non-religious people can relate to—but it didn't matter. He wouldn't touch it because of the way I was introduced.

Being an outspoken Christian in the music industry means always feeling out of place. It's like whatever you have accomplished is less credible because of your faith. You're in the circle, but you're not *really* in the circle. You fit in, but you don't *really* fit in. When you're standing next to people or sitting beside people, it's as if you're not really there.

This is one of the reasons I don't fully embrace the "Christian rapper" label. It isn't that I'm ashamed of being a Christian. I'm not. If someone asked me to renounce my faith or take a bullet in the brain, I'm dying that day. But labeling the music that way creates hurdles and is loaded down with baggage. Plus, it just isn't a true expression of the music I'm making. I try to produce music that is life-giving and inspires people to hope, but it isn't just for the super-religious. I want to address themes that people who aren't Christian can appreciate.

There was a time when I was making music that appealed only to those inside the church. But that day of exclusivity is long gone. My albums will always have my DNA in them, and I will always be a Christian, but I'm trying to do something different now. But for many who aren't familiar with me, this doesn't matter. I'm already marked as a Christian rapper, and maybe I always will be. As a result, whether I'm walking the red carpet or at a party or talking to professional athletes or even having a conversation at the barbershop, I'll always feel tension. I'll always be an outsider.

In nearly every interview I do with the media, people struggle to talk about my actual music. Instead, they want to know if I smoke or drink or cuss. They ask if I feel weird around non-Christians. They want to know if I'm trying to evangelize people. I'm like a caged animal that people want to observe, but they aren't sure how close they can get.

Once while on tour I was visiting a mainstream radio station in North Carolina, and a station operator informed me that they wouldn't air my music: "We really love your sound, but we just don't play Gospel here."

07

"It's not Gospel. It's hip-hop," I protested. "It's just that *I* am a Christian."

The guy couldn't wrap his head around it. He said they had a sister station that played Gospel, but they weren't interested in my music either because "church moms don't want to hear rap."

You don't have to be a rapper who is Christian to understand what I'm talking about. If you're a person of faith who works a regular job, or interacts with your neighbors, you have likely felt this tension. You've probably sensed it at parties, or office functions, or over coffee with non-religious friends. If you're a Christian and you have a pulse, you probably know what I'm describing.

It's like, you fit in, but you don't fully fit in. There is a sameness with those around you, but also a difference. You feel accepted by those around you, but not all the time or all the way. You may have gotten used to it, but it still raises important questions about what it means to be Christian in a world that assumes Christians are obnoxious. Or irrelevant. Or hypocritical. Or judgmental. Or ignorant. Or bigoted. Or any number of negative adjectives.

Looking back, it seems like God has been preparing me to navigate this space all of my life. Ever since I was a knucklehead kid stirring up trouble, I have always stuck out. I've been *like* people but not exactly like them. I've always been from a different place, a different perspective.

I was an artistic kid growing up in an urban culture that didn't know what to do with artists.

I was influenced by the gangstas in my family but didn't have the skill set or desire to follow suit.

I ended up with a theater scholarship to college but didn't fit in with the fine arts crew.

As my single mom and I moved from city to city, I never seemed to find my niche.

Every significant life event, every birthday was a reminder that *I didn't fit in.*

It's as if God had enrolled me in boot camp, and I wasn't even aware of it. It's like God knew that one day I'd need a little extra something to keep showing up when it felt awkward, to keep walking when no one noticed, to keep making music even though many dismiss it before even listening to it.

I didn't win the Grammy for "Best Rap Performance" that year, and I was surprisingly disappointed when my name wasn't called. But in retrospect, I think I received something that was more valuable: a reminder that part of being human—and especially being Christian—means not fitting in, and the only solution is learning to look to God for ultimate recognition.

As I've said in songs and speeches, if you live for people's acceptance, you'll die from their rejection. This belief has made it possible to keep doing what I do and keep being who I am, unashamed.

My name is Lecrae.

I'm not who people assume I am.

I don't fit neatly into people's boxes or conform to people's labels.

I have a troubled past and have made more than my share of mistakes.

A few years ago, I met God and started making music.

Neither of these has made life simple.

I still make my share of mistakes.

I guess what I'm trying to say is, I'm like you.

I'm a lifelong wanderer trying to love God and be who I was created to be.

This is my story.

And maybe it's yours too.

1 -
DADDY
ISSUES

———

Dear Uncle Chris, Uncle Keith, Uncle Ricky,
Before the Lord get me I gotta say something quickly
I grew up empty since my daddy wasn't with me, shoot,
I wasn't picky I'd take any male figure
You stepped in at the right time . . .
I just wanna be like you,
Walk like, talk like, even think like you
The only one I could look to,
You're teaching me to be just like you

Lecrae | "Just Like You" | *Rehab*

———

"Somebody get the doctor in here."

A nurse shouts down a hallway at Houston's Harris County Hospital. She rushes back into the room and tries to calm a screaming woman who is drenched with sweat and gripping the bedside in pain. It's just past 1:30 in the afternoon on October 9. The physician finally arrives, and a handful of heaves and grunts later, a 7-pound-1-ounce baby with a stack of black hair running down the center of his head takes a first breath.

Cradling the child in her arms, the woman looked into the eyes of her new son, Lecrae Devaughn Moore.

And so my story began.

My mom, who goes by the nickname "Tut," had unexpectedly gotten pregnant when she was only twenty-three. She had already broken up with my dad. The two knew they were young and immature, but they decided to get married anyway. That's just what people did in those days under such circumstances.

But my parents' biggest problems didn't stem from their ages; they resulted from my father's abusive personality. He was using drugs and drinking heavily. His unpredictable temper combined with her fiery disposition made for an explosive situation—not one conducive to raising an infant. My mom knew he was one bad trip away from getting really ugly. Before I even reached my first birthday, my mom snatched me up and escaped. I became a fatherless child before I could even pronounce the word *daddy*.

Raising me by herself meant struggling to make ends meet. Between the occasional government assistance and my mom's multiple jobs, we never lacked basic necessities. We always had food on the table. It may have been liver, cheap meat, and government cheese, but the table was never bare. Even if our clothes came from Goodwill, we were never without shoes or shirts. As a result, I didn't realize I lacked the financial means other children had. I knew we didn't have as much as some kids in my school, but I assumed we were like a lot of other normal people.

By elementary school I had left Houston and moved to Denver's Park Hill neighborhood, but things barely improved. Poorer communities in Colorado aren't as bad as hoods in other parts of the country, but they aren't vacation destinations either. Crime was common, and drugs were everywhere. We may or may not have had weed growing in our backyard, and my babysitter may or may not have cooked crack in her kitchen. (Before the "war on drugs," these sorts of things were more common.)

Whatever I lacked in terms of financial resources, I made up for with machismo. In first grade, when most children learn basic addition and subtraction, I knocked a kid's tooth right out of his mouth. In fourth grade, when kids are experimenting with the scientific method, I was formally (but incorrectly) accused by my school administration of gang activity.

13

Part of my bravado was a way to hide the nagging feelings of insignificance as a young kid. My mother and my aunts tried their best to encourage me and tell me they believed in me, but the unspoken forces in the world made me feel like "less than." Even though I wrestled with self-esteem and a lack of identity, I couldn't articulate it. And when I did, others didn't seem to care. So I began to believe that my problems and pain weren't important, that I should keep these thoughts bottled up, which only worked until the anger built up and spilled over onto those around me.

"Why are you always acting out, Lecrae?" my mom often asked me after I had gotten into trouble.

I shrugged my shoulders like I didn't know.

But deep down, I *did* know the source of it all.

★ ★ ★

Underneath all of my pain and misbehavior was a sense of emptiness. After my mom and I escaped my dad's instability, he decided to stay away. And the hole left by my father's absence throbbed constantly, like an open wound that refused to scab over. On a lazy Saturday, my mind would sometimes flood with questions:

> *Where is my dad right now?*
> *Is he thinking of me too?*
> *If so, why doesn't he find me?*
> *Why doesn't he at least call me?*

Countless questions. Zero answers.

Sitting in class, with my elbow propped up on the desk and my head leaning against the palm of my hand, I'd stare out the window and begin to daydream about what it would be like to have a dad around. My imagination filled the hole my father left with romanticized versions of what I thought he would be like.

Lying in bed at night before falling asleep, I'd picture my dad showing up and making our family complete. I could almost hear the knock at the door and could almost see the door swing open. My heart rate increased as I imagined him walking into our home and fixing our problems. He was an absentee father struggling with addiction, but in my young mind, he was a superhero. He had the power to swoop in and save the day, to save me from my confusion and frustration and woes—*if he wanted to.*

I mostly held it together during waking hours. After playing in the neighborhood, when a man's voice would call a friend of mine home for dinner, I wished it were *my* dad calling *my* name—but I wouldn't let others know. On occasion, when no one was around, I would shatter like a windowpane and break down. Tears, tears, and more tears. Telling my mom I wanted to go live with my dad. Asking her where he went and why he didn't want to be with us. She would try to offer answers that painted a dignified picture of him, but it never satisfied.

The years rolled on, but the pain never disappeared. I mourned my dad's absence and yearned for his presence. Every child wants and needs a father, and mine didn't want anything to do with me. No phone calls. No birthday cards. No arm around the shoulder after a bad day at school. (Actually, one call and one card.)

I'm not the only kid to grow up with this pain. Millions of fatherless children in America struggle with this reality. The loneliness. The missing person in the stands when they finally hit the home run. The pain of watching their mothers struggle to bear the burden of a two-person job. The sinking feeling when the sun rises and sets on yet another Father's Day. And, of course, the hundreds of aching, unanswered questions that leave them wanting to scream, "How come he don't want me?" like Will in that famous scene from *The Fresh Prince of Bel-Air* after his deadbeat dad leaves again.

I've heard people say that the traumas from our childhoods follow us into adulthood. That's certainly true for me. If you could trace my life's biggest struggles back to their origin, most of them would lead to a childhood version of me wrestling with my father's absence. Even when I wasn't rebelling or having an emotional break-down, there was a dull, throbbing sense of rejection and abandonment.

Because I felt like my dad valued drugs more than having me as a son, I've constantly wrestled with my self-worth and craved the approval of others. Because I thought the person who should have found me easy to love didn't, I wondered if I was worthy of love. Because he didn't consider me reason enough to stay, I always felt like a disappointment to others. Because my dad's non-existence stirred up so much anger, my temper flared and hurt those around me. And because I lacked a consistent male role model in my life, I had no idea what it meant to be a man.

In the swirling pain of abandonment and insignifi-cance, I searched for someone—anyone—I could look up to. My cousins and uncles filled this role somewhat as the only older males in my life. They were my surrogate role models, but no one filled in the cracks completely. They were more like pieces of a composite dad. Each had their strengths.

My Uncle Keith, for example, was introverted like me and passionate about music. He introduced me to reggae and was always introducing me to new artists. Together we would listen to Yellowman and Marley and all kinds of records for hours on end. My Uncle Ricky was stylish and creative and taught me how to be well groomed. He was always encouraging and affirming, and he actually enjoyed spending time with me. We looked alike, and sometimes when people would mistake me for his son, he'd claim me. My Uncle Chris was as tough as steel, and I drew strength from him. Hanging with him was exhilarating, and I always felt like he had a plan for me.

But unlike the father I wanted, I didn't see my uncles and cousins every day. Some lived close by, but most were half a continent away. I wanted role models who really understood me and never left my side. I wanted role models who spoke my language and were willing to tell me the truth about life.

And this is where hip-hop rushed in like water to fill the cracks left by my father's absence.

★ ★ ★

My first encounters with hip-hop took the form of covert missions. At least, that's how they seemed as a five-year-old. I spent the summers at my grandmother's house with my middle-school-aged cousins. After I was put to bed, my cousins would turn on *Yo! MTV Raps*, an early hip-hop music show. The music would filter under the door like an alarm clock, and I'd spring out of bed. Staying low to the ground, I'd sneak into the living room and peek at the television from behind the couch.

For two hours, the *Yo! MTV Raps* hosts, Ed Lover and Fab 5 Freddy, would introduce videos by the likes of Ice Cube and A Tribe Called Quest. The images were mesmerizing. One of the first music videos I saw was by Eazy-E and featured a kid who looked like I did. The language, scenes, and sounds felt familiar, but embellished. It made my world seem glamorous and attractive rather than unfortunate. It was instantly relatable.

On Saturday mornings, I'd wake up before anyone else and go to the living room to watch cartoons. But one

17

morning I discovered a channel that played rap videos early on Saturdays. From then on, there was an internal battle about what I should watch. Some mornings Bugs Bunny would win. Other mornings, Nas came out victorious. But over time, it wasn't a contest. I went straight to the hip-hop.

When I returned home to my mom's house, I wasn't able to watch MTV because we didn't have cable, so I sought it out other places. I'd borrow tapes from friends and even watch the free previews for the pay-per-view music channel over and over.

My mother worked at a halfway house, and sometimes she would take me with her when she had to work late. Whenever the former inmates would rap at the table, I observed and took mental notes about their style and song choices.

"Here you go, little man," an old resident whispered to me one day.

He reached into his pocket, pulled out a mixtape cassette, and slid it across the table to me.

It might as well have been a $100 bill. I played that tape on repeat—day after day after day. I memorized every lyric from every song by every artist he included—N.W.A., Beastie Boys, LL Cool J. It was all I wanted to listen to. The music consumed me.

As I aged, hip-hop became a regular part of my life and not just something I encountered once in a while when no one was looking. My mom always played music in the house. As I grew older, she joined in and played more commercial rap like MC Hammer.

My friends and I began hunting down rap videos and emulating what we saw on television. We'd sing the songs and try to replicate the outfits. In the afternoons, my cousins would put down cardboard in the front yard and break dance in their old school Adidas jogging suits. They would pop and dance and have rap battles with other kids in the neighborhood. By the time I was eleven or so, all my free time was filled with listening to music and watching videos. Like most of my friends at the time, I had no aspirations other than being a rapper. No doubt. It was going to happen one day.

My obsession with hip-hop stemmed from more than my love of music. It also filled the vacuous cavern left by my father's absence. When I was younger, not having my dad was like losing a security blanket. Without him, I didn't feel fully safe or fully loved or fully wanted. But it became painful in a different way as I aged. I didn't have anyone to teach me to shave or talk to me about women or answer my questions about what it meant to grow and mature and act responsibly. There was no one there to say, "I know what you're going through; I've been there." Young boys need their fathers to model and teach them what being a man means, just like girls need mothers to help them grow into women. Without any constant male role models, hip-hop artists became my heroes.

This is actually a common social phenomenon in poor communities where fatherlessness is rampant. As one African-American writer who grew up with an absentee dad wrote, "In the late 1980s and into the 1990s, the answer [to fatherlessness] for many of us was hip-hop. Nowhere was there a more ready supply of black men with something to say and the ability to articulate it in a way that allowed others to relate and learn than in the booming hip-hop culture. For young black men in search

19

of guidance from someone with a face that looked like their own, rappers became the surrogate fathers."[1]

Tupac became my second parent. He was sort of like my mom and my favorite uncle wrapped into one person. My mom was passionate about cultural empowerment, and my uncle was a gangsta. When loneliness grew heavy, when I needed advice or direction, when happiness morphed into sadness, I'd listen to Tupac. Unlike my father, he was always there for me. I could trust him.

On days when I felt the sting of abandonment, I'd play his track called "Papa'z Song" which might as well have been written with me in mind.

I rarely spoke about my traumas, but Tupac seemed to speak about them for me. He gave voice to *my* angst and frustration, *my* life and situation. Tupac was so special to me that when he was killed, I wept while watching his funeral procession on television. It was almost like my actual father had died.

For those who grew up in a rural town with both parents or in a comfortable suburban community where your biggest concern is what time Applebee's closes, my relationship to hip-hop might sound a little far-fetched or silly. But it makes perfect sense for those who were raised in the inner city during that time.

When I was a child, most people feared urban communities and the people who lived there. "White flight" was taking place in cities across the country, and this meant that many cultural influencers—filmmakers, authors, journalists, preachers, teachers, politicians—didn't understand those of us without the means or desire to leave. Whenever politicians and TV preachers talked about inner-city neighborhoods, they often promoted

20

stereotypes. Television and film rarely projected images of black youth in these communities unless they were criminals or fit certain stereotypes. The implicit message from culture to kids like me was that the world wasn't made for me, or at least didn't understand me.

This disconnect to the broader culture was further intensified by an inner-city culture that encourages hardness and machismo. A kid in the hood couldn't just sit around whining about wanting a daddy or family unity without being laughed at or told to toughen up. Yet somehow rappers like Tupac and Ice Cube got away with it. And this brought kids like me relief.

Hip-hop gave me hope that even though I felt alone, I wasn't. It reminded me that there is often a difference in the value people ascribe to you

HIP-HOP GAVE ME HOPE THAT EVEN THOUGH I FELT ALONE, I WASN'T.

and your actual worth. It told me that my pain was valid. That even though I wasn't speaking of my struggles, they were worth discussing. And at a time when I didn't feel heard or seen, hip-hop made me feel significant.

★ ★ ★

As time progressed, the music sank deeper and deeper into my soul. But things got real when the music started to flow back out of me.

Throughout grade school, I didn't feel like I had much to offer society. In the hood, the way you form your identity is to find something you're good at and then form a mini-community with other people who are good at the same thing. But unlike other kids, I wasn't the star any-thing. I wasn't good at fighting—my scrawny frame wasn't going to scare anyone off my turf on the playground. I wasn't an athlete—I wasn't interested, and anyway, there was no one to take me to practice. I wasn't the most intel-ligent—I wasn't flunking classes, but I wasn't headed to Harvard either. I wasn't stylish and fashionable—we didn't have enough money for me to hang with the best-dressed kids.

So there were kids who played basketball and kids who jumped rope and kids who solved math problems. I was only good at hanging out. At after-school programs I'd run around on the playground and goof off with the other hanger-outers, but I lacked any cultural currency or credibility. I felt like I had nothing . . . but then I signed up for a talent show.

The Boys and Girls Club ran an after-school program that I attended during grade school, and they decided that the kids needed something to show off their gifts. I remember there were a lot of dance groups. I wasn't a part of one of those, but I knew I could rap. So I signed up.

I liked performing, so I was excited to have an oppor-tunity to prove I was good at something. I decided to do Naughty By Nature's "O.P.P.". Every morning during the week leading up to the talent show, I would stand in front of the mirror and sing into my comb. I practiced my moves and my facial expressions. By the time the day arrived, I owned it.

My name was called, and I was introduced.

| *Deep inhale. Slow exhale.*

And then I let the music out. The cadence, the tone, the pitch was perfect. I was dancing and singing and rapping. Halfway through the first verse, I looked out at the crowd. People in the front were bouncing from foot to foot. Slowly it spread, and then people were feeling me. Their cheers grew.

The praise fueled me to perform harder, to dance faster, to rap better. I had listened to the song so many times, I probably could have sung it in my sleep. It was all muscle memory now. My pulse quickened. Adrenaline rushed. My face beamed, but I was locked in. Euphoria.

Suddenly, kids were slapping their hands over their mouths and shaking their heads in disbelief. I heard one yell, "Oh, shoot. Is that Lecrae? I didn't know he could rap." And when it was all over, they erupted in applause.

Like I said, where I grew up, one's currency comes from what they're good at. From then on, kids would ask me to rap on the playground. The brave ones would challenge me to battles, but no one could beat me. I practiced at night to make sure I'd be on fire when the time came.

My social status rose at the Boys and Girls Club, but the deeper longings remained. Childhood inched toward adolescence, but in some ways I remained that baby boy born in Harris County Hospital a handful of years prior. I was still crying out for attention, nourishment, and love. I didn't have athleticism or toughness or fancy clothes or the highest intelligence. I didn't

> SOME OF LIFE'S STRUGGLES ARE SO SEVERE THAT EVEN MUSIC IS POWERLESS TO OVERCOME THEM.

have a father at home or any consistent role models to show me what growing up looked like.

But at least I had the music.

Music was my everything. It was my escape. It was my medicine. It was my therapy. It was my identity. It was my companion. It was my sanity. In the face of so many problems, music was my salvation.

Well, almost.

Some of life's struggles are so severe that even music is powerless to overcome them.

2 -
NOWHERE
TO RUN

———

I'm tryna act like it ain't real
Had my innocence just stripped from me
And I still don't know how to feel
And I'm wondering how to address it
Can't tell my family, too messy
So I just embrace it, it's hard to face it
I'm too ashamed to confess it
So I kept it in and ain't speak
Didn't think, it hit me so deep

Lecrae | "Good, Bad, Ugly" | *Anomaly*

———

The beer can whizzed by my head. Luckily, I had good reflexes as a child.

That day had been a particularly emotional one. School was putting a hurting on me, friends felt hard to come by, and everything I did seemed to get me in trouble.

My mom and I got into it over something stupid, and her boyfriend at the time decided he would step in and tell me what was what. Rage and sadness mixed until tears ran down my face and I erupted like a volcano of emotion: "I want my daddy!"

In one smooth motion, mom's boyfriend cocked his arm and hurled the beer he was drinking at me. As the aluminum cylinder rotated end over end, time slowed like in *The Matrix*. I bobbed to the right, and it barely missed my face.

"Your daddy had you, and he left you," he yelled.

These words sliced through my self-esteem and reopened the wounds left from being abandoned by my father.

That's right, I thought. *My dad* did *leave me. And probably for good reason. Who would want a punk like me anyway?*

The scene was not an uncommon one. I was constantly assaulted by sharp-edged words—phrases that could cut deep and leave me limping for days. An ancient king once wrote, "The words of the reckless pierce like swords, but the tongue of the wise brings healing."[2] I encountered far more of the former type of words than the latter.

At the slightest sign of weakness, friends and family would call me a sissy or a punk or worse. And they usually said it loud enough that others could hear and shame me too. I felt like I was called belittling names almost as much as "Lecrae." No matter the frequency, it was enough to cast a shadow on my childhood.

When I became an annoyance—like most kids do from time to time—only a handful of people ever explained what I was doing wrong or how I could improve. When I misbehaved, no one stopped to show me a better path. When I failed, no one consoled me or told me that this was a natural part of life. Denigrating and demeaning words abounded.

I sometimes felt like many of the people I loved didn't love me back, and worse, they were tearing me down with their words. This alone is enough to mess with a kid's mind, but it didn't stop there. I lived under assault, and the abuses were not just verbal.

★ ★ ★

"Lecrae, come into my room."

They seem like harmless words, but they changed everything for me.

I was six years old and staying at a babysitter's house. My mom was working late to keep food on the table, so various family, friends, and neighbors had to watch me during the week. This particular day, my babysitter was a seventeen-year-old girl. I was playing with some toys in the living room when she called me down to her basement bedroom.

27

When I walked into her room, she closed the door behind me. Her voice was lower than normal, and her face looked different. She pulled her pants down, and I saw the female anatomy for the first time.

"Come here."

I trusted her. She was an adult, and adults could be trusted, so I did what she told me to do.

It goes without saying that I was exposed to things no child should ever be exposed to. Even now, it's painful to think about the explicit details of what I was asked to do.

"Alright," she said afterward. "Don't tell anybody about this. Go back and play."

I walked out of her room, and the door closed. But when the lock clicked behind me, it was like a door to another world opened in front of me. It was a pathway out of innocence. It was as if I had eaten from the forbidden fruit tree and received all sorts of knowledge. I knew that what I had just experienced shouldn't have happened, that something wasn't right about the whole thing.

It happened a few more times, and I started to think that something was really wrong with the whole experience. An alarm was going off inside of me. So I tried to tell my mom what happened, even though I wasn't able to fully articulate it. She said she would deal with it.

Years later, when I was writing a song with a verse about it, I asked my mother how she had dealt with it. She didn't remember what she said to my babysitter, but the sitter denied anything happened. Whatever she said, it worked. The situation changed, the abuse stopped, and it was never brought up again.

There was less knowledge about these matters back then. Few knew the importance of reporting child sexual abuse to the authorities, or making sure a child received counseling to process the abuse appropriately. I didn't want to tell a soul about the abuse or attempt to cope with it. It reinforced my sense of aloneness and helplessness. And it left my mind spinning from the massive download of new information that no child of that age should have.

Prior to these encounters, I didn't know what a naked female body looked like, and to be honest, I never considered that it might look different from my own. And most impactful was that I didn't know I could do something to create such an intense and bodily reaction in someone else. As a child who wanted to feel loved, to please others, to be good at something—this felt good.

My brain was rewired, and I now believed that I was supposed to physically pleasure girls. When other kids were watching *Sesame Street*, I was trying to get girls somewhere and get their pants down. In closets. On beds. In basements. Not having reached puberty myself, I wasn't able to have sex, but I was still having regular sexual contact. I was growing comfortable with fondling girls—girls in my neighborhood, friends from school, even girls I was distantly related to.

It wasn't that I had become a sexual deviant. I was just mimicking what I had been exposed to.

When I was eight, I was running a race at a school field day. My teacher stood at the end cheering me on. I ran right through the finish line and buried my face in her crotch. She pulled me away, thinking it was an accident. But it wasn't accidental. I was recreating what my babysitter taught me to do.

Not only did the experience sexualize me, but it gave me a new language. A secret code that only others with similar experiences can understand. Children who have been molested develop something of a sixth sense that helps them identify other victims. In conversation, you would use words and hear words that only those intimately familiar with the anatomy of the opposite sex would know. The victims would identify each other in these conversations even though none of the other kids realized what was happening. Once you identified each other, you would end up messing around and fondling each other. It became a thing among those of us who

29

were part of this community of the afflicted. We were all messing around with each other, but no one was talking about it to those outside the group.

Sometimes I hear from fans that are living with experiences similar to mine. My advice to them is always the same: say something. Life on earth has sharp teeth. It has a way of wounding us. The only way to begin nursing your wounds is to name your wounds.

There are few guarantees in life, but you can count on this: *if you ignore your wounds, they will not go away.* They will get worse and grow infected. And when an infected wound is ignored, the infection can spread to other parts of your body, to other parts of your life. There's no shame in speaking about the traumas of life. It's just admitting that you're like everyone else. What happens to you doesn't define you. But it can kill you if you ignore it.

Of course, acknowledging your wounds is not the solution—it is only the first step in it. Healing is a process—the kind that moves inch-by-inch, year-by-year, often spanning a lifetime. I'm still uncovering new layers of injury that need renewal and repair.

I didn't have the courage to talk about my wounds at the time, and as a result, I sank deeper into darkness. Each encounter gave me brief sensations of what felt like intimacy. It almost felt like love. I wanted to mean something to someone, and at that age, no one had responded to me with emotion outside of an occasional pat on the back. The emotions were warped, but they were real. I had been sexualized at a mere six years of age, and there was no stopping me now.

★ ★ ★

My legs peddled as fast as they could, but they were outpaced by the beat of my heart. I hadn't told my mom where I was going before I left, and she was surely worried now. I needed to get home as fast as I could and put out the fire.

Whizzing into the driveway, I jumped off my bike and was met by my mother's boyfriend. I tried to explain what happened, how I lost track of time and didn't expect to be gone so long . . . POP! The full force of his hand collided with my face, and my body collapsed. My hand touched my face, and I realized he had snapped my nose bloody. Everything was a blur after that.

He wasn't the only person in my life who vented their anger physically. Members of my extended family would smack me for misbehaving or just to mess with me. Once an uncle locked me in the trunk of a car and drove around town. It wasn't that the people in my life who hurt me were exceptionally evil or didn't care about me. Many of them were products of similar behavior and were carrying on the cycle started generations earlier.

Where I grew up, no one really spoke about it as "abuse" either. In fact, I'd never considered it that until I was an adult. It's nothing for a kid to be smacked or slapped to the ground for misbehaving, and older kids hurting younger kids for sport is common. It's accepted as an inevitable, if not normal, part of life. On boring Saturday afternoons, other kids and I would trade war stories about our experiences.

"One time, the man who my mom is with hit me with an extension cord," I'd say.

31

"I got beat with a jump rope," another would respond.

"Yeah, well my mom beat me with a water hose," a third would say.

We would talk about being beaten and talked down to without any idea of how these experiences were impacting the young men and women we were becoming. None of us realized that each act of violence was training us to perpetuate the cycle when we were grown up and could graduate from abused to abuser.

The effect of these things ran deeper than I could have imagined. It wasn't until I had my own kids that I could see the potential dangers. Sometimes I react the only way I know. And though I would never physically abuse my family, I can react with anger rather than love, and my wife has to help me see that I'm replicating the behaviors modeled for me. In these moments I have to stop because, as a father, I see the potential dangers this kind of past can cause. I've had to learn that my natural responses aren't normal, that the only way to live a future that's better than my past is to cling to God in the present.

Domestic violence was also common among adults. A drunk husband might slap his wife for no reason. A sober one would do the same just to vent his pent-up aggression. Luckily, in our house, this was not a problem among the grown-ups. Only a very stupid man would try raising his fist to my mom. She was nobody's victim. When it happened, she fought back and won. Other women in our neighborhood, however, were not as strong or as lucky.

This quiet culture of abuse remained mostly in the shadows. It was dragged into the light only on occasion, when rage lost all constraint and things went too far. For me, a plastic spatula ushered in that day.

An infant family member was playing with it and accidentally hit herself in the face. She started crying, and my mother's boyfriend assumed I had hit her. I told him I hadn't touched her, but he didn't believe me. I was so prone to lying that I wouldn't have believed me either. Except this time I was speaking the truth.

After some back and forth, he told me to go to my room. But as I was walking up the stairs, my sense of justice got the better of me and I turned around to face him.

"Only God knows the truth," I shouted.

A look of fury that I had never seen before came over his face, and I panicked. He rushed toward me, and I turned to run away. The attempt was futile, and he caught me at the top of the stairs. Grabbing me by the arm, he pulled his arm back swiftly as if to crank a lawnmower and hurled me down the stairs. My body tumbled uncontrollably, each rotation sending shocks of pain through my spine. I landed on my side at the landing, the wind had been knocked out of me on the way down. Rolling onto my back in an attempt to catch my breath, I looked up and saw that he was not done punishing me for my defiance. He tore down the stairs and was seeing red now.

Leaping over the last few stairs, he landed on my chest and pinned me down. Left hook, right hook, left hook, right hook. He was swinging full force, and it was the first time I remember ever fearing for my life. I saw only flashing lights and heard only the sound of my mother screaming for him to stop. Finally, my mom ran to the kitchen and rushed back with a plate in her hands. Smashing it over his head, a shower of porcelain rained down around me. He fell back, and I crawled away.

33

The next thing I remember, police officers were standing in my living room and my mother's boyfriend was in handcuffs.

For a time, I was happy. He was gone, and it was just mom and me again. But that was not to last.

A knock at the door, and my mom walked into my room: "Lecrae, someone is here to see you."

The door swung open, and there he stood. Her boyfriend was crying and apologizing and had a Sega Genesis video game console tucked under his arm. I looked at my mother, and it was clear she wanted me to take him back. I didn't blame her. She wanted companionship and couldn't afford to keep the house up without help. I did not want him back, but I wanted her to be happy, and I wanted the video games.

Life at home was different after he returned. I had zero interaction with him. We didn't speak, and we didn't fight. We became just two people living under the same roof. He knew better than to mess with me, and I knew better than to mess with him.

The pent-up frustration and anguish began to build and boil. My mind started filling with rage and apathy. As the anger I'd stuffed away bubbled up, I started trying to become a fighter. I'd pick fights for every reason and no reason at all. I grew intrigued with gang culture, idolizing the way they provided community and toughened up their members.

I began running away from home a lot, which revealed the hopelessness of it all. Each time I ran away, it wasn't long before I realized I had no place to go. Where do you run when you have nowhere to go? Home is the place where kids can go when they are hurting and afraid and confused. But I had nowhere.

★ ★ ★

Sometimes I hear people talk about growing up in a gated community with a mom who cut the crust off their sandwiches and a dad who coached Little League, and I don't know how to relate.

The verbal, sexual, and physical abuse I experienced was a three-stranded rope that wrapped my neck like a noose. It was not just squeezing out my innocence and my joy, it was also crushing my sense of faith. Like many of my peers, I lost my faith in the ability of others to take care of me. I lost faith in family members, those people who normally form the anchor of children's lives. And in some way, I think I lost my faith in faith.

In a trauma-filled world like mine, God was an after-thought. God was irrelevant. If God did exist, and I had my doubts, He wasn't looking out for people like me. So why would I waste my time looking for God?

Looking back, I wish I knew then what I know now. I wish I knew that I was still valuable and lovable. I wish I knew that my dignity was not determined by my circum-stances but burned into me before birth. The events that happened to me violated my dignity, but they didn't remove it. At the time, I didn't know any of this. But I do now.

Years later, I sat down to write a song called "Good, Bad, Ugly" and decided to do what I wished I had done as a child: name my wounds. I talked about the abuse and the pain and the confusion and the fear I experienced. But then I transitioned to something even more important

35

than the wounds; I talked about the potential for those wounds to be healed:

> *And only God can help me get free*
> *But I've been forgiven, my Savior risen*
> *I'm out the prison, I know that*
> *I got the power to say "no" to all of my struggles*
> *God will control that*
> *Every time we slip and we fall*
> *Gotta get back up and fight on*
> *We are not defined by our past*
> *The future look bright, I see the light on*

Fans often write me to share their emotional reactions to this song and the hope I share at the end. They didn't know they could shed their shame. They didn't know they could get rid of their guilt. I make a point to show off my scars because I want others to know that they aren't alone.

Talking about wounds is important, but talking about our healed wounds is just as important. Because scars are the evidence that wounds can heal. That wounds don't last forever. That healing is possible.

TALKING ABOUT WOUNDS IS IMPORTANT, BUT TALKING ABOUT OUR HEALED WOUNDS IS JUST AS IMPORTANT.

Today I'm able to talk about what happened out of a place of hopefulness and healing and comfort. I didn't know that healing was possible, and I sure didn't know where to find it. I was just a lost and troubled kid who wanted to be a rapper.

3 -
A
FRAGMENTED
LIFE

———

Teach me to do the things that men do
True,
You showed me stuff I probably shouldn't have seen,
But you had barely made it out your teens,
And took me under your wings
I wanted hats, I wanted clothes just like you,
Lean to the side when I rolled just like you
Didn't care if people didn't like you,
You wanna bang, I wanna bang too
Skyline Piru
You would've died, I would've died too

Lecrae | "Just Like You" | *Rehab*

———

For most kids, summertime means the end of school and
the beginning of sleeping late, swimming long, and staying

up past bedtime. For me, the arrival of summer meant leaving home.

After school wrapped up each year, my mom would send me away by plane, train, or automobile to stay with my grandmother in San Diego for several months. To someone who grew up in a home where children never left their parents' sides for extended periods, this may sound a little odd. But my mother's decision to send me to San Diego was made *for* me, not in spite of me. Mom despised the idea of accepting government assistance, so summers gave her a chance to get in front of her finances for the next year. With me gone, she could pick up some late-night shifts and work a second job.

My mother wasn't the first one in our family who needed to send her kids to a relative's house. My grandmother often did the same with her when she was young. My mom actually thought her aunt was her mother until she was old enough to know better. In many poor communities, family members have to help each other pick up the slack by watching each other's children. So spending my summers at a relative's home was not as strange as it may sound initially.

My grandmother's real name is Georgia, but everyone calls her "Big Momma." She is a tough and resilient woman. As one of sixteen children in a poor East Texas community, she learned in childhood to literally fight for a seat at the table. Some of the men in Big Momma's life didn't treat her well. But she persevered, eventually taking responsibility for raising twelve children.

A devout Christian, Big Momma is the one who first introduced me to faith and religion. Big Momma's parents—Bishop Bryant and Mamie—had a radical transformation in the Holiness Church of God in Christ, so they were not just regular Christians. They were the on-fire, Pentecostal, tongues-speaking, Holy-Ghost-baptized kind of Christians. Bishop Bryant and Mamie had strict moralistic rules for their sixteen children and expected them to be in church whenever the doors were open.

By the time I was born, Big Momma was carrying on the spiritual legacy of her parents. She is generous to a fault, and when she meets someone in need, she makes it her personal mission to help. She would often take me down to the food bank or a shelter where we stocked up on essential items to distribute to the community. Her garage and the shed in her backyard were always brimming with clothes, bread, baby formula, and other necessities. Everyone in the neighborhood knew that they could come see Big Momma if they needed anything.

39

Once a month, Big Momma would wake me early in the morning to make dozens of sandwiches. We'd load them into her car and take them across town to hand out to homeless people who lived under a bridge. If we weren't going to shelters or helping the homeless, we were going to senior centers or nursing homes to visit the elderly, who would make sure to fill my pockets with peppermints.

Once my grandmother met some Christians from Mexico in San Diego, and next thing I knew, we were handing out food and clothes at Spanish Pentecostal churches. We couldn't understand what they were saying, but we went anyway. This led to Big Momma connecting with Brother Santiago, a minister from Tijuana. From then on, if the mood hit Big Momma right, we would hop the trolley to Tijuana or even travel to towns deeper in Mexico where we would serve poor people there.

I didn't fully understand what all this faith stuff meant at the time, so I tried to make the best of it. Our trips to Tijuana became opportunities for adventures. One time, I decided to play a joke on the border patrol and crawled under a blanket with just my feet sticking out. When they saw my tiny ankles, they waved us over and investigated us. After asking me to recite the Pledge of Allegiance and perform some other tests, they decided I was likely American and let us go. Big Momma was not amused.

The amazing thing about Big Momma's ministry is that she didn't wait for a mission team to assemble or apply to a sending organization. She just went where she knew there were needs and found ways to meet them. Though I didn't realize it at the time, Big Momma was showing me what it means to be a Jesus-follower and make sacrifices in the service of loving one's neighbors.

40

WHATEVER I SAID MADE HER BELIEVE I WAS PROBABLY A CHRISTIAN, BROTHER SANTIAGO BAPTIZED ME IN THE PACIFIC OCEAN.

Big Momma may be a natural missionary, but she was never trying to beat me over the head with her Bible. The closest she ever came to pushing anything on me was when we stopped at the San Diego Bay on a return trip from Tijuana. She and Brother Santiago walked me toward the water and then asked me a series of diagnostic questions about whether I believed in God and Jesus. When whatever I said made her believe

I was probably a Christian, Brother Santiago baptized me in the Pacific Ocean.

Of course, Big Momma wasn't just a mission-minded church lady. In addition to all the religious work, we would also go to the zoo, fair, or beach. Some afternoons we would ride the ferry to Coronado Island where all the rich people lived. When I was young, she would put me on her back and carry me around the house. She made sure I had fun while I was there.

When I tell stories of spending my summers as a child roaming freely around San Diego and having sleepovers with cousins and friends, people tell me it sounds like paradise. But I've only told you part of the story.

★ ★ ★

Big Momma lived in the Skyline Hills neighborhood of Southeast San Diego, which is one of the poorest and most notorious parts of the city. Things got so bad there that in 1992 the city officially banned the name "Southeast San Diego" in all communication because it had become synonymous with crime, drugs, and poverty. (There is a *Gangland* episode about this neighborhood, if that tells you anything.)

Most of the homes there were built in the 1950s or '60s and—though they were maybe one thousand square feet on average—were often crammed with residents. The house to our right had seven people living inside, and the one to the left had six people. Down the street was a foster house that had a rotating group of residents with tons of kids.

Big Momma was the undisputed matriarch of our family. Her house was like the family motel; everyone stayed there at some point. I have eleven uncles and aunts and many more cousins, so there was no telling who would be waiting when I arrived. Her house had three bedrooms and an enclosed patio. I usually slept with one or two other family members on the patio, which doubled as a church on Monday nights.

There were two types of people I never remember seeing in Skyline Hills: tourists and white people. At some point there were probably plenty of white people residing there, back when it was a desirable place to live. In fact, I'm sure the first black families who settled there thought they were moving up in the world. But after white flight, the situation shifted.

By the time I was spending my summers in Skyline Hills, the neighborhood had deteriorated. Shootings were a common occurrence. I got used to seeing obituaries and funeral programs pinned up on the walls of people's houses. More than one of my uncle's friends was killed in a drive-by. One of our close family friends was mowed down too. It devastated our household. But, at the same time, it also felt somewhat normal.

There was a canyon down the street from Big Momma's where the other kids and I would ride our bikes and have rock fights. One day I was playing in the canyon with some friends, and we stumbled across a dead body. It was the first time I had seen a corpse. We stood over it for a minute talking about it and then went back to goofing off. We never told the police or anyone else because we didn't think a murder was significant enough to report.

In contrast to the dead body, the streets of Skyline Hills made me come alive. This is where I felt like I had a chance to be somebody, to be a part of something bigger than myself. And it was just fun. I spent my days scouting new music at the "Fam Mart" and playing for hours at the public swimming pool. But more than anything, I spent my time on the streets stirring up trouble. I'd steal from stores, throw rocks at windows, sell food stamps for money at the corner store, and ride my skateboard while hanging onto the back of the ice cream truck.

The kind of trouble I was used to was mostly childish stuff, but when I hung out with my Uncle Chris, things got real. He was fun, talkative, and loud. He was the life of the party and a magnet for mischief. When I was still in elementary school, Big Momma would often ask Chris to watch me while she ran errands.

43

Not wanting to be stuck in the house, Chris would take me on adventures with him and introduce me to new things along the way. He let me sit in his lap and drive his car when I was seven. He would set up fights between me and other boys in the neighborhood to toughen me up. When Chris would go hang out with his girlfriend, he would try to get me to hook up with her little sister. Sometimes he would take me to the drug house, and I would sit outside and whistle if the cops drove up.

Uncle Chris even showed me a gun for the first time when I was only eleven years old. We had been cruising down Imperial Avenue in his freshly waxed Chevy. He told me how he had made some serious money doing some things that could've gotten him arrested and gave me a talk about how life works. Pulling the car over, he leaned over and released the glove box door. Reaching in, he pulled out a black 9 mm and held it in front of my face. I was mesmerized.

Uncle Chris made Southeast San Diego's streets look sexy, and over time, he became my chief role model in California.

He was tough; I was weak.

He was an extrovert; I was an introvert.

He fit in; I felt like an outsider.

He seemed to know who he was; I had no idea.

The problem with wanting to be like Uncle Chris was that he was heavy in the streets—drugs, violence, and all that. He was also a pledged member of Skyline Piru, a set affiliated with the Blood gang. A "set" is like a franchise business, and like actual franchises, they come and go. Some sets will actually go out of business over time. Or they'll shrink so low that they might as well disappear. Skyline Piru was a big set and a revered set. And it was thriving.

Skyline Piru came into their own in the 1970s, but they were revered in Southeast San Diego throughout the '80s and '90s. To put their influence into perspective, a single police bust of Skyline Piru in 2009 resulted in 93 arrests as well as "19 guns, 240 marijuana plants, 10 pounds of harvested cannabis, about 20 pounds of powder and crack cocaine, two pounds of methamphetamine, 18 vials of PCP, some 3,000 ecstasy tablets and roughly $60,000 in cash."[3]

I was hungry for male attention, and Uncle Chris offered a father-like relationship. I was hungry for acceptance, and Uncle Chris symbolized the promise of a family-like community. And I had idolized gangsta rappers like Tupac and Ice Cube and movies like *Boyz n the*

Hood and *Menace II Society*. Uncle Chris seemed like the living embodiment of everything my heroes sang about. Hanging with him was like seeing all my heroes up close. Gangs have ranking systems, and I'm not sure where Uncle Chris fell, but it felt to me at the time like he was at the top. The more I idolized Uncle Chris, the more he drew me into his world. He was proud to have someone revere him, and he was raising me to be like him.

So Southeast San Diego was, for me, a place where two worlds collided. There was Big Momma's world of Christian compassion, church services, and short-term mission trips to Tijuana. And then there was the world of guns, gangs, girls, drugs, and adventure. Had I been forced to pick between them, I would have chosen the streets every time.

The movies I had watched, the rap songs I'd been listening to, the stories that Uncle Chris told me—they all made me feel like it was my destiny to join a gang and become like so many others. But even though the streets were made for me, I soon found out that I was not made for the streets.

45

★ ★ ★

Inner-city neighborhoods have an anatomy. The type of person you are determines the role you play. The divisions between one part and the next are not always clearly marked, but everyone knows where the boundaries are. When kids are young, they don't play a role. They just stick to whatever their siblings or closest friends are. But when young adulthood arrives, everyone gets sorted like in *Divergent*. You become the part that best suits you, and you play that role. As I grew older, I noticed five major roles I could possibly assume.

A *gangsta* must be an active gang member. Once you prove you're committed to the family, even willing to kill for it, you're allowed to join. Gangstas are responsible for holding down the block. They have to "put in work," which might include tagging up a wall with graffiti and marking it with the gang's name, robbing someone and bringing in money, or taking out an enemy. Unlike other roles, this one is not extra-curricular or optional. The "gang life" is a way of life.

Perhaps more than gangstas, I admired the *pimps* and *hustlers*. Maybe it was the old '70s movies like *Super Fly* and *The Mack* that embellished these roles in our community. If you had a knack for manipulating people, and making money, you became a hustler. And if a hustler was especially skilled at controlling women, he became a pimp.

Our community also boasted a few talented *athletes*. Everyone was proud of people who filled this role, so the community made sure athletes stayed out of trouble and away from drugs. When I was spending summers in Skyline Hills, Byron and Peebo were two athletes I admired. They were amazing ballplayers, and we all rooted for them.

As far as my friends and I were concerned, if you didn't fit any of the other roles, you were an *OJ* or "Ordinary Joker." These people are almost invisible. They often stay in their houses or at least their own yards. No matter what I became, I determined not to be an OJ.

As a kid, I spent most of my time with gangstas because of my Uncle Chris. Since he saw the world through a gangsta's lens, he wanted me to become tough and aggressive. He would make me confront kids who stole from me or picked on me. He would make us scrap like pit bulls until one of us was bleeding and didn't want to keep going. I got beat up a lot until I learned to fight a little.

As my elementary years wrapped up, other kids started to gravitate toward gang life, and the stakes went up. Playing football in the streets and skateboarding behind the ice cream truck morphed into actual gangbanging. I stole a gun out of a neighbor's garage so I could have my own. I ended up hiding it in a tree so Big Momma wouldn't find it.

But as the stakes rose higher, my interest in being a gangsta dropped lower until it was clear that this wasn't the role I would assume. More than any other category, being a gangsta requires commitment. After some OGs in the neighborhood challenged me to be ready to kill or be killed, I questioned if I was committed enough. Most of my friends were Skyline Piru members, but I didn't know if I wanted to be initiated.

47

My friendship with four boys who lived next door to Big Momma made me further question whether I wanted to follow in my uncle's footsteps. Their dad was a music minister in a local church, and he did all he could to protect them from the streets. They weren't allowed to leave their front yard and barely left their house. Typical OJs. Other kids in the neighborhood made fun of them—not just because they were sheltered church boys, but also because they were talented musicians and songwriters. Their dad was training them to play instruments, and even though their musical skills would be impressive to many, no one else in the neighborhood gave them any respect.

After I discovered I was good at music in the Boys and Girls Club back in Denver, I began to quietly show up at their house to learn from them. We would spend hours writing songs together. I was good at writing lyrics and rapping, and they would compose music to accompany it. But I was embarrassed to be hanging with artistic kids like them, so I hid our friendship from everyone else. But every time I left their house having created some fresh music—living, breathing songs and lyrics—I felt there was something more for me than gang life could provide.

Realizing that I would never become the thing I spent years trying to become led me into an adolescent identity crisis. I wasn't tough enough or committed enough to be a gangsta, not physical enough to be an athlete, and not boring enough to become an OJ. Looking back, I think with my entrepreneurial spirit I could've made it as a hustler. If I had seriously gotten caught up in dealing drugs or chopping up cars, I probably would have taken off. But I never fully pursued it. So there wasn't *any* place for me in California.

And worse, there wasn't a place for me back in Colorado either.

★ ★ ★

Early in elementary school, my teacher back in Denver started to notice I was different. I was an excellent student early on—earning me the nickname "Straight-A Lecrae"—and no longer being challenged by the standard curriculum. So my teacher called a conference with my mom to recommend a side program for gifted students that was being developed. My mom agreed.

For the first time in my life, I was given a space where I was encouraged to be creative. For an hour each week, they introduced us to brain exercises and word games. And they also carved out time just to be expressive. Each class, I was given time to draw and write. In fourth grade our teacher introduced us to poetry. This experience, combined with the freedom to explore music I found after owning the talent show, awakened something inside me.

By fifth grade, the teachers who ran the gifted program told my mom that I was excelling. They informed her that I might be a candidate for a new arts magnet program at another school. My mom discussed the option with me, and I was skeptical. If I followed the path most of my classmates were taking, I would go to Martin Luther King Jr. Junior High. Everyone knew that's where all the good-looking girls were. But my mom, who always valued educational excellence, convinced me to try out for the program anyway.

I agreed. I auditioned. I got accepted.

The program was set up like college. My major was theater, and my minor was creative writing. I loved these classes, but the program was hosted by an inner-city school across town. So each day a bunch of creatives were bussed in from other communities and descended on this downtown school.

Just like in Skyline Hills, I found myself in the epicenter of two opposing worlds colliding. The artistic kids who were in the program with me were interested in poetry and literature and theater, but what I experienced in Skyline Hills was also true here: the environment didn't value these things. The arts were uncool, embarrassing, stupid, weak. So I ended up shunning a lot of my artistic

49

friends outside of class and trying hard to fit in with the other kids instead. I hid the artistic side of me because I didn't want to be made fun of. I wanted to fit in.

When kids start living divided lives, it affects them. One minute they act like one person and the next another person. Soon they begin to forget who they really are. This isn't just the way kids work; it's the way humans work. But it's worse when you're young. You long to be someone. So I felt like I had to choose, and I decided to reject the artistic side. After my sixth grade year, I begged my mom to take me out of the arts program and let me go back to MLK Jr. Junior High School with my friends. After some begging and pleading, she agreed.

Having spent my entire childhood both wanting desperately to fit in and having never found my place, I went into a tailspin. My grades fell even further. MLK Jr. Junior High was ranked one of the worst in the state, and it ended up being featured on *Nightline* because of its low performance. In the segment's B-roll footage, I was shown running down the hall, jumping and slapping people in the head.

I started getting in fights at school, and not just harmless ones. I stomped a dude in the hallway one time, and he wasn't even fighting me. In the back of my mind was the shame from losing so many fights in San Diego. I was on a mission to prove I wasn't soft any more.

Life also was unraveling at home, where my anger was spilling over. I was like a bomb that could explode at any moment without warning. My mom and I fought all the time, and we'd end up in raging scream matches for almost no reason at all. I was regularly smoking weed by then, and she was frustrated with all the trouble I was getting into.

TAK·N OFF

neckkce

YouNG Black aNd wreckflace/Schemin on a
teachers told me that I wasnt nothin but a
detrinent/ lookin up to my uncles threw them
knuckez @ they faces/yah I know I rap
but I seen em pumpin base/caught a
case I was 15/ MoMA think In Psxboo/
me I wanna be PAc All my homiez wanna
be Michael/ Park Hill, GreenValley/I was in
those bellos too/ Famly on the East Side so
I wanna be Soo woo!!/ head them disisters a
the coppers look for choppers/ I was hangin
on the block I aint wanna be no doctor/
thank the LoRD FoR my MoMA She Shown
me better options /I was ent
Thought I was Goin no where
see me now & I aint stoppin

One Saturday afternoon, I was walking through the
neighborhood with a bunch of friends. One of my bud-
dies pulled out a BB gun that he brought from home. I
couldn't believe how realistic it looked. The metal was
cold like a real gun. Smelled like a real gun. It was even
heavy like a real gun. It reminded me of Uncle Chris's gun.

I asked my friend to let me hold it. My fingers gripped
the handle and tightened, releasing power and adrenaline
into my veins. Now I was the one with the gun. I was like
Uncle Chris.

I joked about holding people up to see if they would
fall for it. My friends laughed, but I was serious. Oncoming
traffic flew by us, and the impulse was too much. My heart
beat faster.

I charged into the road, pointing the black pistol at a
car heading toward me. The woman inside the car locked
eyes with me. My heart was pounding, but I didn't show my

anxiety. My face was solid and serious like a kid who was just stupid enough to pull a trigger and murder a stranger.

Panic flashed across her face, and she slammed on her brakes. Smoke and screeches poured from her car until it stopped a matter of feet in front of me. The whole block smelled like charred rubber. I could see the terror in her face as she froze, paralyzed from fear. I had all the power.

Tears streamed down her cheeks, and her hands shook as she inched the car backward. She thought she was going to die, which is exactly the way I wanted her to feel.

Once she was gone, I doubled over laughing. My friends couldn't believe what had just happened. It was as if I had won the prank of the year. Nobody had the guts to do what I had just done. I had earned respect.

More than their admiration, I loved the sense of power it gave me. So much of my life was spent being the victim, but in that moment, I was in control. Nobody could bring me down.

Within a few minutes, an unmarked police car swooped in on us. They threw us on the ground, knees in our backs, and cuffed us. After detaining us, questioning us, and realizing the gun wasn't real (and that we were minors), they drove us home. My mom was mad, but she wasn't surprised. It was nothing for a cop to knock on our door at night, having picked me up for vandalism or trespassing, or even waving a BB gun at oncoming traffic.

By the time high school arrived, I felt like I had nothing. I had lost my dream of being the second coming of Uncle Chris. I had lost the chance to grow as an artist in a specialized educational program. And I had lost hope that my dad was ever going to return home and be the man I needed in my life. I didn't know who I was. I only knew

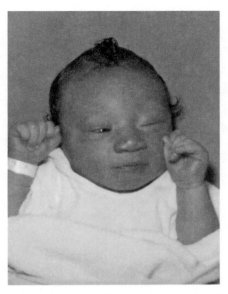

My first picture at Harris County Hospital in Houston. Fresh out of the womb, I was already sleeping with one eye open.

My third birthday with my cousin, Julius, in Denver. We were like brothers. I was cuter though.

As we moved from city to city,
I never seemed to find my niche.

My mom, who goes by the nickname "Tut,"
and me in my church clothes.

Some times Bugs Bunny would win. Other mornings, Nas came out victorious. But over time, it wasn't a contest. I went straight to the hip-hop.

Raising me by herself meant struggling to make ends meet. We never lacked; she always provided.

As a four-year-old at San Diego Bay. Big Momma baptized me in the ocean there.

My uncle thought it was a good idea to let his two-year-old cousin hold his can of Old English beer.

In the swirling pain of abandonment and insignificance, I searched for someone—anyone— I could look up to. My cousins and uncles filled this role somewhat as the only older males in my life. They were my surrogate role models, but no one filled in the cracks completely. They were more like pieces of a composite dad. Each had their strengths.

My Uncle Chris was like the Dad I thought I wanted.

Whatever I lacked in terms of financial resources, I made up for with machismo. In first grade, when most children learn basic addition and subtraction, I knocked a kid's tooth right out of his mouth.

Big Momma would carry me all the way into adulthood. She helped raise me to be more than I could have been on my own.

Sitting on Big Momma's lap.

My fifth grade photo. I asked my mom
to cut my hair in "a Gumby."

My mother was always good at making the most of every occasion. She could use a little to make a lot.

Outside Big Momma's house. The easy access to the roof made for plenty of trouble with my cousins.

After graduation from high school. To this day, my Aunt Shirley is a huge supporter.

College allows you to make better decisions, better friends, and a better future. There's only one catch: when the opportunity comes, you actually have to take it.

that I didn't fit in anywhere and that I was miserable. But just when I thought it couldn't get any worse, an unexpected opportunity arrived that I thought might change my life for the better.

★ ★ ★

Ever since we'd moved from Houston to Denver, I'd hoped that one day we'd make it back to Texas. I thought Denver was a dead end for me, and I was ready to get out. I imagined I'd have an easier time finding my way if we lived down South. We finally got the chance during my freshman year of high school. My stepdad was working at a restaurant, and people saw he had a knack for accounting, so he began to rise in the ranks. A job opened up in Dallas, and management offered it to him.

The original plan was to move to Duncanville, a black suburb south of downtown. But before my mom would agree, she needed to go scout out the school system. She refused to sacrifice my education in the move. When she asked people around town about the quality of schools, she discovered that Duncanville schools weren't that great. She wanted to go to the north part of Dallas. That settled it.

The day we moved into our new home was a proud one. It was a typical one-story ranch-style house, but it was a mansion to me. Sure, we didn't have hardly anything inside, but we were in a very nice neighborhood. I thought I was ballin'.

Then reality set in, and I realized that while this North Dallas suburb may have had the best schools, it barely had any black people. So here I was, a black transplant who had spent his entire life living in an urban context, stuck in the middle of a place where no one looked like me, talked like me, dressed like me, or listened to the same music I did. I had only had one white friend before moving, but now that was all there was. The isolation, depression, and despair that I'd hoped to leave behind in Denver had followed me to Dallas.

Out of that pain I lashed out by acting like a hoodlum. I finally found another black transplant who lived a fif-teen-minute walk from my house, and we became as thick as thieves. We looked for trouble everywhere we went, always trying to channel the hood life in the middle of this land of strip malls and chain restaurants. I went back to braids and the red clothes typical among Blood gangs. But my effort to find my place only made me feel more alone.

The weed mellowed me out a little, but the high was always temporary. I was stealing from stores, but I always ended up with something less than what I really needed. So I started drinking more heavily, trying to flush the loneliness away. Or at least drown it out. But this didn't help at all. Each night of heavy drinking was followed by a day wracked with a headache and all the same emotions I'd experienced before I'd picked up the liquor bottle the day before.

When substances failed to help, I tried to invest time in new activities, thinking that a change of pace would solve my problems. A coach suggested I join a sports team, but basketball proved to be a poor substitute for what I really needed. I still didn't know who I was and even had people call me Devaughn (my middle name) in an attempt to give myself a new identity. People had always made fun of my name anyway, calling me "Lecrap" or "Lecrusty" or joking that I ate my dinner on a "Letray." I figured if Lecrae couldn't find a place to fit in, maybe Devaughn would have more luck.

Women were the next type of object I used to cope. *Maybe I could find acceptance in someone's arms or between someone's sheets,* I thought. So I started dating heavily, trying to find my identity in the context of relationships. I was having a lot of sex, sometimes with more than one person at the same time. Women were only as good to me as the pleasure they could offer. I started running through them left and right.

One afternoon at an amusement park, I randomly hooked up with a girl. Days later, my urine was burning.

"Son, it appears you've contracted a sexually transmitted disease," the doctor told me.

He might as well have punched me in the stomach. How could this be? Luckily, he said, it was chlamydia, which was easy to cure with a round of antibiotics. But the situation was more complicated than that because after my hook-up at Six Flags, I'd had sex with one of the star female athletes at school. She called me because she had also gone to visit the doctor, and when he explained that her stomach pain was from an STD, she knew I had given it to her. She was livid.

My life was spinning around me, and everything was a blur. I was no longer just depressed; now I was scared of what the future held. I began doing some soul searching, asking questions about the existence of God and life after death. The way I was living, I might have to face those two sooner rather than later, so I figured I better prepare either way.

One day I eavesdropped on a conversation in one of my classes between a Christian girl, Izehi, and an atheist named Chris. Izehi was telling him all about Jesus and God and the Bible. He responded that there was no God and we were all just taking care of ourselves. This is a pretty standard atheist belief, so it shouldn't have shocked me. But I was such a mess at this point that the thought of being responsible for my own life was mortifying. If I had to take care of myself, it was a wrap. I didn't want to become like the Bible-toting Izehi, but I couldn't accept that what Chris was saying was true either. So I set out to figure it out myself.

I started spending time in the library, researching books on religion and philosophy. I hit all the isms: Hinduism, Buddhism, Judaism, Mormonism. I finally asked my Muslim friend, Jamin, about his faith. The way he described Islam made sense to me. Their spiritual practices were pretty straightforward, and they had a book that laid out all the rules. Jamin gave me a Quran, and I started studying it at home. I even went to a mosque with him once. A month later, I gave this religion up too. In Islam, my standing with God depended on my efforts to be righteous, and I was sure I couldn't live up to that standard. Plus, even if I could, there was no guarantee at the end that I would get to heaven anyway. You just had to hope that you had been righteous enough for Allah to accept you once you died. I decided to stay in the "undecided" category for now, and keep investigating.

When my senior year arrived, I felt like something—maybe God—was breaking me down. I wrote poetry and music to express myself, and the words started changing. They were richer, more personal now, no longer just rap clichés and empty rhymes. They became tools to help me wrestle with who I was and why I was on earth. My worldview began to crack, and my thinking deepened.

Sports, sex, substances, and soul-searching had all failed to bring me the fulfillment I wanted. I had searched for answers to life's most important questions, but they always seemed just beyond my reach. The same sense of aloneness I felt as a child from being abandoned by my dad was still there, half a layer below the surface. The restlessness inside made me feel like I was going to explode.

And then one night, I did.

I had been regularly running away from home, and my mom was at the end of her rope. Just after sunset, she said something that struck a nerve. I screamed in pure Tupac fashion: "It's me against the world. I hate this life! I'm out!" I told her that I had always wanted to go to a downtown school, that my terrible grades were her fault because she brought me here to begin with.

"You're acting just like your daddy," she finally shouted, "and that's why I left him."

Her words were like a brick thrown through a fragile window. All of the hurt of my childhood and adolescence—the rejection, the confusion, the rage—rose to the surface. Tears filled my eyes. Angry tears. Walking into the bathroom, I flung my neck forward and head-butted the mirror. Glass rained down.

57

Mama + DADDY would fight @ home
haules / I know nothin different
so I screamin back you make
me [strikethrough] who [strikethrough] the kitchen / AND
I'm ITCHIN just + HIT the doc
[strikethrough] cause this
here's CRAZY / [strikethrough]
RADIO SMEBODY SINGIN How they
hate they lady /

I picked up a shard and climbed on the roof. Holding the glass at my wrist, I screamed that I hated my life and wanted to kill myself. I shouted my pain into the sky for anyone who wanted to listen: my parents, the neighbors, even God if He existed.

This was not just some cliché, empty threat made by a teenager who wanted some attention. I might have tried to kill myself before now, but I thought that was the weak way out. That constraint was now gone. I thought, *If this is weak, I'm going to be weak today. I've punched holes in doors, and I've punched people's faces. What else can I do to get rid of my frustration?* I felt like every breath I took was a waste, and I didn't want to take any more.

I was one move away from bleeding out on the rooftop of my house. But with the glass pressed against my wrist, something held me back—*hope.*

It was faint, but it was there. I had hope that someone, someday would come save me from all this. I don't know where the hope had come from, but it had been there all of my life. Deep down, I held this belief that someone—maybe my dad, I don't know—would show up and rescue me. *If I could just hold on.*

My terrified mother tried cussing me off the roof. When that didn't work she yelled, "Stay up there then. Imma call the police on yo' crazy behind." The cops arrived shortly after and convinced me to come down. I walked into my room, adrenaline pumping, throwing any object within arm's length. Flinging myself on the bed, I grew quiet and my mom entered. She was calm now and holding a black leather book.

"Nothing I'm doing is working. Nothing is helping you," she said. "Right now, only God can help you."

She placed a Bible next to where I was sitting. I paused for a moment, unsure of how to respond. Finally, I picked it up and walked toward her.

"I hate the Bible," I said, bending back its cover.

Gripping a stack of pages, I began to rip chunks of paper out and throw them into the air. They fell into piles around my feet. I tried to destroy the only thing that could rescue me.

RIGHT NOW, ONLY GOD CAN HELP YOU.

My mother shook her head and left. There I was, standing alone, staring at the tattered paper and shattered glass that was scattered across the house. It was more than a mess; it was a metaphor for my fragmented life.

My mom was right: Only God could help me now. But I didn't realize it at the time because I was still blaming others for my problems and still telling myself that I could solve them all if I just worked hard enough.

If you don't know you're lost, you can't be led. And if you can't be honest, you can't be healed. Before I could be rescued, I needed to realize I was stranded.

59

4 -
LOST MAN
ON CAMPUS

Where am I going? What I'm living for?
I rolled the dice on life so tell me what they hittin' for it
I'm three shots in, probably depressed
But crying about my problems ain't gonna get me out this mess
Ride around playing Scarface, I'm a hard case
I want to die, but I'm scared of looking in God's face
Popping pills and powder, trying to kill some hours
Cause when I'm sober, man I promise I can feel the power
Of death eating me slowly I'm on my way
Heaven or Hell? Well that's only for God to say

Lecrae | "Devil in Disguise" | *Church Clothes 2*

Sometimes life hands you an opportunity to do better, to be better, to correct your course, to carve another path. For millions of young people each year, going to college offers one of these big breaks. It's like hitting the reset button on life. No one knows what you've done or who you are. You can take all you've learned as a child and teenager and construct the person you want to be. College allows you to make better decisions, better friends, and a better future. There's only one catch: when the opportunity comes, you actually have to take it.

I started thinking seriously about the possibility of college after missing curfew one summer night before my junior year of high school. I was supposed to be home at midnight, but it was at least two in the morning when I opened the front door. Cellphones weren't really popular yet, so my mom and stepdad had no idea where I was and no way of finding out. The frustration had built by the time I arrived with my friend Bryan—and both of us were as high as kites from smoking weed.

The door swung open, and my mother stood there. Only this time she didn't look angry—she looked exhausted. Fed up. I'd worn her down with all the drinking and drugs and trouble making. We'd been in Texas for about a year, and the list of trouble I'd gotten into was long. I'd been arrested once, I'd stolen my mom's car and crashed it into the neighbor's house, I'd picked a fight with a Mexican gang that resulted in some members coming to our house and shooting up my stepdad's car, and I was under investigation for being affiliated with a theft ring that was robbing apartments in the area. When I didn't come home, it could have meant anything. I could be dead in a ditch for all they knew. Tonight she didn't have any fight left.

"No one knew where you were, Lecrae. We were worried," she said, shaking her head. Turning toward her bedroom, she looked at my stepdad: "I don't know what to say right now. You talk to him."

My stepdad motioned for Bryan and me to sit next to him on the couch. He looked at the ground in silence for a moment, trying to think of what to say. My stepdad didn't have a father growing up, so he didn't know how to have a father-son style conversation. Plus, we had a tense relationship in which he never really offered me advice. So when he finally found the words, it got my attention:

"Lecrae, can't you see that the way you're living is not taking you anywhere?"

He pointed at the room.

"Look at this house. Do you want to own a house? Because at the rate you're going, you're never going to own a house like this," he said. "You're not going to be able to pay your bills. You're not going to be able to provide for a family. You're not going to be able to do anything. You're not going to amount to anything where things are headed. If you keep this up, you're going nowhere."

With that, he got up and went to bed. I never said a word back to him.

Bryan cracked a couple of jokes, and then we crashed too. But I couldn't fall asleep. I couldn't get my stepdad's talk out of my mind. He didn't chew me out or even raise his voice. He just took the time to tell me the truth. And he was not just anyone; he was a man. Without a father, I never had many "man-to-man" conversations or even had men speak to me so seriously. As I lay awake, his words echoed in my sixteen-year-old ears: "You're going nowhere." He was right. No doubt. I didn't want to end up an aimless wanderer—like my dad.

Oh shoot, I'm going to ruin my life, I thought. *Maybe I should get it together.*

63

The coming months were turn up time. I started thinking about how I could start making improvements and get my life straight. The problem was that I didn't have any examples of what this looked like. My friends were as messed up as I was. The only positive images I could think of were Fresh Prince or Theo from *The Cosby Show*. So I decided to channel that. *WWTD: What Would Theo Do?*

The only answer that kept popping up was college. My mom had always been big on education. She was the first woman in our family to go to college, and she often reminded me that I needed to go to college if I wanted to really make it in life. At first I figured I should probably go to Howard University because, well, that's where Diddy went. I started to apply and then figured how much it would cost me to go there. So Howard was out.

Then I heard about a program called InRoads that was committed to empowering minority youth in Texas. They helped kids get internships and apply for jobs and stuff. Each year, they took a group of kids on a college tour to a bunch of state schools. I signed up, and off we went.

This trip turned out to be one of those times when God really worked on me behind the scenes. I was asking big questions about life and identity and what was really important. Along the way, the bus stopped at a strip mall with a Christian bookstore in it. We had time to kill, so I walked inside. It felt strange, like a craft store that your grandmother might shop in. But off to the side was a CD section, and I needed some new music. Most of the albums looked cheesy, and then one by a group called Anointed caught my eye. The album was titled *Under the Influence,* and I knew something about that. So I bought it.

I threw it in my CD player, put my headphones on, and hit play. The lyrics were surprising. Rather than angst and darkness, they were positive. The music felt like the neo soul sound being popularized by Erykah Badu. Listening to it made me feel good about life. The title song became my soundtrack for the rest of the trip.

> *Love without condition*
> *This is my addiction*
> *It's a need that only God can fill*
> *Once I got to taste it*
> *Nothing could replace it*

Each campus we visited had its strengths and weaknesses. I liked the University of Texas because it felt as big as the state itself. I wanted to be a part of something big. I didn't care for Texas A&M because it felt too nice and clean and conservative and buttoned up. Texas Southern impressed me because it had the girl factor. Then I went to the University of North Texas, and I really liked it because it had the most black students for its size. There were so many people who looked like me and talked like me and wore similar clothes to mine. I could envision myself there.

When I got accepted to the University of North Texas, I thought my opportunity had come. On my campus visit, I discovered they offered a full ride to students who qualified for a theater scholarship. I had rejected the artistic side of myself for so long, but the skills were still there. I auditioned with a piece from the play, *A Raisin in the Sun*. I could tell by the looks on the theater professors' faces that I had slayed it.

That settled it. I was now headed for the University of North Texas with tuition paid in full by the theater department. My opportunity had arrived, and I was going to seize it. Or so I thought.

Old habits die hard, and if you're not careful, the person you used to be can overtake the person you're trying to become.

★ ★ ★

One word describes my first day on campus at North Texas: intimidation.

Imagine being an introvert surrounded by thousands of strangers all playing by rules that you haven't learned yet. This was my shot, and I was afraid I was going to drop the ball. I could hear all my friends growing up calling me a punk. I could hear my mother's voice telling me that college was the way out. And I could hear my stepdad's voice saying, "If you keep this up, you're going nowhere." I remembered that my biological dad never got past eighth grade, and I sure didn't want to turn out like him.

I lived in tension from the beginning. On one hand, I wanted to fit in and be a part of the social scene. I'd craved a community, a tribe, my whole life and thought this was where I'd finally find it. But I also wanted to do well academically. I knew that graduating from college meant I'd have a better chance at success in life.

The thought of a fresh start got my blood pumping. I changed my name back to Lecrae and tried to mind my business. I avoided asking a lot of questions or looking like I was out of place. I just wanted to blend in. But from day one, I was off my game.

My first roommate was a tall, skinny white dude. I'd never been in such close proximity with such consistency with a white dude before. He didn't respect my space, so that didn't go well. After I caught him in my bed with his girlfriend, I had enough. The situation quickly grew tense, and he asked for a transfer by the end of the first semester.

Since my roommate wasn't going to be my best friend, I had to look elsewhere to find people to hang with. Within weeks, I'd sized up the way the campus operated and analyzed the different groups just like I had back in Skyline Hills. An outsider couldn't tell who's who from just walking around campus. But if you went to the Student Union around noon and paid attention, you'd see people break up into groups.

The most popular students held court in the middle. This was mostly made up of the fraternities and sororities. All the energy came from the middle. I immediately knew I couldn't be a part of this group because I didn't have the money to be a member of a fraternity. And, freshmen can't pledge for historically black fraternities anyway, so it wasn't an option for a year.

Just outside of the middle were the athletes. Having played basketball in high school, I thought I might gain access to this crowd by walking on. But after one workout with the team, I knew it wasn't for me. I wasn't going to wake up at six o'clock every morning, eat a bunch of protein, and run until I felt sick in *hopes* of making the team. College was supposed to be fun, not lame. So that wasn't going to happen.

On the outside fringe were the artistic students. Being black and artistic meant you were a very, very rare breed. It was almost impossible to be both. The arts community—theater, dance, music—was mostly white at North Texas. So if you were too artistic, black people looked at you like you were white. While I had to embrace the arts for my scholarship, I decided to reject the community. I was afraid of being an outcast, and all I knew was black culture anyway.

The only people who could float between groups and break the system were those who were just exceptional. People who were exceptionally funny or exceptionally well-dressed, or exceptionally well-connected, or had a personality that drew attention. I didn't have the money to wear the best gear, and I was shy, skinny, and trying too hard to be funny.

Here I was again, stuck without a seat at the table. Was this going to be the theme for my whole life? Was I destined to be an outsider?

Before I got to feeling too low, I discovered another group of people on campus. You wouldn't find them at the Union in the afternoon. They didn't care about fitting in with the aristocracy like the others. Instead, they could be found outside Crumley Hall—smoking Black and Milds, leaning against a Caprice Classic, blasting bass from twelve-inch subwoofers in the trunk. Arms marked up with tattoos and branded symbols. Gold teeth flashing. The hood crowd just stood around—congregating outside like most had done in their neighborhoods back home.

To some people, it might seem strange that these kids were on campus at all. Most of them were in the first generation of college students in their families. They grew up with parents telling them that they needed to go, so they went.

But they didn't know how to succeed once they arrived. No one had gone before them to show them the ropes and mentor them through it. They reverted to what they knew. Because you can only be what you've seen. And you can only become what you've beheld.

Because we came from similar settings, the hood crowd felt more comfortable to me. I thought back to my childhood hero, Tupac, and the way he was tough and authentic to his roots while still allowing his poetic side to come out. He had different layers like I did, so I thought maybe I could be dynamic too.

The difference was that Tupac was able to blend the many facets of his personality into a single person. At North Texas, expressing both sides of myself meant compartmentalizing, not blending. Barely into my first semester, I started to fracture once again.

SAT outside my college class
Smokin blacks / hoodie black / I aint
sposed to be in here / these people wanna
hold me back / Dont no one believe in
me cept family & my boppin Coach /
only men I looked up too thought all this
rappin was a joke / auntie, told me learn my
way shoot for education / but you use ur
mind aint gotta shoot for education /
idolized the dope gate / gangsta sellin cocaine /
what Im up in school fo / got me feelin so
lame / promise I'm backwards in my thinkin
and identity / cuz all these gangstas die
young and aint even half the man they
prentend to be / Texas on down Tennessee /
ignorant with no remedy / thank the Lord
He picked me up / and showed me I had
dignity.

Because I foolishly read the clock

I'd hang out with the hood crowd when it was convenient, when I wanted a familiar setting. But I was never all of "me." When I needed a creative outlet, I'd hang out with the artistic crowd, but almost never in public. We'd hang out in dorm rooms, but I wouldn't be caught dead sitting with them at a table in the cafeteria. Another identity crisis. I was two separate people, but neither really knew who I was. *Should I wear Polo today, or FUBU? Should I grow braids, or keep my hair short? Should I listen to Outkast, or Cash Money? Should I roll dice, or check out the play on campus?*

One day I was standing in the Union in the middle of the day all alone. I wasn't standing with anybody because I didn't have anyone to stand with. And that is when it hit me: college created the same dynamic and lack of acceptance I experienced back in Dallas . . . back in Skyline Hills.

A sinking feeling overcame me, and I felt the cloud of depression roll in. I thought college was my chance to finally find acceptance, but it turned out to be another letdown.

I went back to some of my most reliable companions: women, drugs, and alcohol (though it was a little harder to come by alcohol as a freshman). When life gets low, people start grasping for things that will lift them up. I always reached for girls first. My sense of value largely hinged on whoever I was with at the time. Sex was always a part of the relationship, but the sex felt even emptier than before. When I had a pregnancy scare, I started to think that women would ruin me.

I smoked a lot of weed, but only in spurts. I was scared to death that I would fail my classes and let my mom down. My mom, a woman who will tell you exactly what is on her mind, would often say to me, "I'm not taking care of no babies, and I'm not going to visit nobody in jail. So you better finish school." Whenever my grades slipped, I would stop smoking weed and start taking NoDoz and pulling all-nighters to make sure I didn't fail. When I got good grades on a couple of quizzes, I'd let my guard down and start smoking again. The problem is that weed made me paranoid, so I'd soon feel a crippling weight on my shoulders again. I'd stop smoking and refocus. Then another good grade or two, and I was back to the weed. I smoked with everyone—white friends, black friends, hood friends, dorm friends, artistic friends, even one of my professors. I had entered an endless cycle that earned me a 3.5 GPA my first semester but left me exhausted.

When I wasn't smoking weed, I was selling it. This started when I bought too much one time and a friend purchased what I didn't need. I started making a small amount at first. Then twice as much, then three times as much, up to nine times, depending on how much I was smoking myself. It was not chump change for a college freshman. Here I was, barely into my first year of school, and the wheels were already coming off. I was smoking weed and selling it, seeking fulfillment from women and feeling empty, trying hard to fit in and failing at it.

My life felt all too familiar. So much for a fresh start.

★ ★ ★

My college experience began with an appetite for new experiences. But by the end of my first semester, there was a tastelessness in my mouth. I had tried everything, and

71

nothing satisfied. Nothing filled me up. I was supposed to be changing my life, but it was all the same. The ecosystem of college looked different from the outside, but it was identical on the inside. It was just a bunch of cliques filled with people who were all trying to be like each other. And like always, I was standing on the outside looking in.

The only difference is that now I knew what solitude really felt like. I thought I had experienced loneliness after my dad left, but I always had my mom. I thought high school felt alone, but in a public high school your teachers and counselors are still holding your hand a little bit. In college, you are really on your own. My mom wasn't there to look out for me, my professors didn't care if I flunked out, and what few friends I had were busy trying to manage their own lives.

It all came to a head one Friday night. My heart had just been broken by a girl I was dating a few hours away at a college in Oklahoma. I tended to guard my heart with women, but in our long, late-night phone conversations, I had opened mine to her. I was vulnerable. When word got back to me that she was talking to other guys, I was crushed. To be fair, I hadn't been fully faithful to her either. But that didn't lessen the pain. I still had no close friends, and none of the people I knew had invited me to be a part of their plans. Bored out of my mind, I couldn't stand the thought of spending another night alone.

Someone told me there was a party at a frat house down the street. I didn't really want to go, but I was out of options, so I went anyway. When I tried to enter, an upperclassman standing next to the door lowered his arm: "What are you doing, bro? This party is invite only."

I looked inside and saw my friend, Nate. *How come he got invited but I didn't?*

I turned and headed back to the street. Across the road from the frat house, I could see some kids playing pool inside a building. They were nerdy freshman kids. The kind that wear their dorm keys around their necks, don't know how to talk to girls, and are math tutors in their spare time. They would definitely have been OJs back in Skyline Hills. It occurred to me that even the lamest kids on campus had something to do tonight. What did that make me?

I arrived on campus aiming for greatness. My hopes were high. But I was starting to think that I would never find my place here. Or anywhere else for that matter. This wasn't a season; it was a pattern.

I started walking down Maple Street with no destination in mind. Where do you go when you have nowhere to go? Everything around me—from the groups of friends laughing to conversations spilling out of open windows to empty beer cans I kicked along the sidewalk—were reminders that I was the loneliest person in Denton, Texas, that night. Even the stars above my head had somewhere to hang. I was more like the darkness around them.

Empty.

Sometimes God lets the darkness settle before He pierces it with light. And that's what happened on my miserable walk that night. Because the light was about to show up and change everything.

5 -
TAKE ME
AS I AM

—

They tell me come as I am but I smell like smoke
My whole life's full of sin cause it's all I know
The Bible told me that you died for my sins
If I believe in Christ, it'll save me from the end
But I'm scared to ask you, to save me my heart
So evil, I got thoughts, that's full of hatred hurtin' people
I thought at first I had to clean up my life
Now I'm hearin' I just need to cling to the light
I'm ready to do it, but Lord I pray you understand
My life is a mess, will you take me as I am

Lecrae | "Take Me As I Am" | *Real Talk*

—

Two headlights appeared next to me, illuminating the asphalt ahead. The face inside the beat-up Cutlass was difficult to make out at first, but when I heard him call my name through the open window, I knew exactly who it was.

Art Hooker helped lead Move, a ministry for black students that met on campus. Sometimes, when I was really desperate for something to do on Monday nights, I'd show up at their events and Bible studies. Art took an interest in me the first time I walked in, and since no one else seemed interested in me back then, it made an impression.

There was a Bible study portion each gathering, and even though I wasn't a Christian, I had experienced enough church that I figured I could fake it. But I was surprised at how much I didn't know. I thought I'd heard it all, but I was encountering stories for the first time. I'm like, "What? Who is this Elijah person, and why is he killing all these prophets? I've never heard of all this." I didn't believe all of it, but I liked that they were philosophizing, asking big questions, and challenging each other. I started to realize that maybe I didn't know as much about Christianity as I assumed. Also, the people who came weren't lame like I thought Christians were. They didn't look unpopular or dress weird, and some of them were really cool. Over time, I kind of enjoyed going, but it was still more social than spiritual for me.

After the meetings, everyone would hang out and socialize and tell jokes. Following one session I went to, the guys got in a circle and started rapping. It was kind of like being back in my old neighborhood in Denver, except the words they were using were different. They were more positive, not centered on sex and drugs and violence and usually mentioned God and faith. I thought it was cool, so I jumped in with one of my own songs.

I kept thinking, "Don't cuss, don't cuss, don't cuss," and changed words like "rival" to "disciple" so that it would be "Christian-friendly."

Art's head snapped to the side. "Man, that was really good," he said. "You can rap."

Over time, I realized that Art was pretty artistic himself. He was a writer and produced some plays on campus. There were few other people outside of my theater program that I could talk with about plays and music and stuff.

Art was also the social coordinator. He would throw parties on campus. They were Christian with names like "Praise Party" or "Holy Ghost Party," and I'm thinking, "What in the world is this?" But I went to one, and it wasn't lame. In fact, it was kind of a scene. It threw me off. Everyone would be hanging around just like the other parties, but they weren't getting drunk or high. They had their own songs and vocabulary. They would dance and tell jokes, and it was actually fun. I thought of it like drinking non-alcoholic beer—it had a similar flavor to something I liked, but some of the contents had been stripped out. Same taste, different effect.

Because Art was artistic and social, I looked up to and respected him even though I didn't know him that well. And that lonely night when his car pulled up next to me, his voice couldn't have been a more welcome sound.

"Yo, Lecrae. You okay?" Art asked.

"I'm fine."

It was clear I was lying.

"You know, Lecrae, I've never asked you this before, but what do you believe in?" Art asked.

"Not really sure," I said. "I know Christians are hypocrites, but I'm looking into a lot of religions."

Art told me that he thought there was an event coming up that would be perfect for a person like me. It was called Impact Conference, and it was in Atlanta. The attendees were people who looked like me and thought like I did. They were really accepting, he said, and I might find a tribe there that I'd fit in with.

It sounded like utopia. At that moment, nothing was more appealing than finding a place to fit in, but he didn't even need to sell me on that. He had me at "Atlanta."

If there was a black Mecca in America during those days, it was Atlanta. Lots of artists were being birthed out of that city. It was the era of Outkast and Jermaine Dupri and So-So Def Recordings and Freaknik. With all the big historic black colleges there—Morehouse and Clark Atlanta and Spelman—there were lots of young people too.

The city also was known as a place where diversity was encouraged and valued. I'd heard it described as the New York City of the South. Everywhere else I'd lived, the black community all looked the same. But in Atlanta there was a wider diversity than other places. The city seemed to me like the kind of place I could really be myself.

I told Art to count me in. One way or another, I was going to be in Atlanta when that conference kicked off.

* * *

Before I went to college, my mom told me not to get a job so I could focus on my grades. It sounded good, but there was one big problem: if you don't have a job, you don't have money. I ran through what little money I brought to college in the first month. I blew the money I made selling weed on a football jersey, some shoes, and more weed. Since it was right before Christmas break, everyone had gone home. My clientele had dried up. And with no money, there would be no trip to Atlanta.

With no options left, I was forced to join the other kids from the ministry who were putting on a car wash. I couldn't imagine anything more uncool than standing on a street corner holding a sign asking people to help fund a mission trip. The only thing that made it bearable was sharing the street corner with this cute girl, Darragh, that I'd had my eye on. Between this and the other kids' fundraising, we collectively raised the money to scholarship my trip.

A few days after Christmas, we loaded a bus bound for Atlanta. On the ride down, I was not saying anything that would reveal who I really was. I just observed them instead. They played strange music for hours and hours.

It reminded me of the Anointed album I listened to on my college tour—not great, but not horrible either. Lyrics that pointed to something deeper than just drugs and guns. But somehow it was making everybody on the bus really excited. People are singing and laughing and getting into it. I'm thinking, "I may not love this music, but I'm hungry for whatever is making you all so excited."

After we pulled into the downtown Atlanta Hilton, I went into people-watching mode. Thousands of black students from across the country had poured in. There were people from D.C. and Baltimore and Milwaukee—I didn't even know black people lived in Milwaukee. There were former gang members with bullet wounds and braids. There were some guys from New York who seemed to radiate electricity. There was a group of rappers who called themselves Cross Movement. They were the best dressed and had an impressive level of swag. There were step teams and preppy kids and people who looked like they had more books than friends. People with different clothing styles and hairstyles and accents. Just like Art said, there was diversity beyond the ethnicity. Oh, and the girls were on point too. This was going to be fun.

After checking into the hotel, we had to select which sessions we would attend. I chose the ones that had to do with urban culture. There was a talk on hip-hop by a rapper. I didn't even hear what he said; I was studying him the whole time. He wasn't a soft pushover Christian guy. He was cool and he seemed like a serious musician. The most impactful session was about sex. I had never heard a Christian perspective on sex, and since I was having a lot of it, I could relate. The speaker said that our bodies were valuable. That they were temples of the Holy Spirit, and sex means sharing your temple with someone else. I'd never connected spirituality and sexuality before. And I had never heard someone talk about how valuable I was.

At night, my roommates would converse about God and wrestle with the tough questions until the early hours of the morning. They talked about Adam and Eve, dinosaurs, Noah's Ark, who Jesus was, and why we were all on earth to begin with. I'd listened quietly and would occasionally comment. These were all the questions I'd been asking too, but they actually had answers and explanations that made sense. I was encountering undiluted truth for the first time in my life, and truth has a way of breaking down a hardened skeptic like me.

The most impactful experience for me was what I kept observing while walking around between sessions.

This was the one place I'd been that wasn't divided into fenced-in cliques. Everyone embraced everyone else. It wasn't a big fashion show with a bunch of peacocks strutting around or a toughness contest where everyone was trying to prove they were harder than the next guy. It was just a bunch of college students who had come to this city to learn and grow and foster love for each other. This was the kind of community I had always dreamed about. I could feel the camaraderie and unity.

For me, everything was leading up to the talent show the second night. I hadn't heard anybody rapping that I couldn't beat, so I was confident this would be my time to shine. The opening acts were all mediocre—a lot of singing, a few step teams, and one terrible rapper. One of the guys from Cross Movement did a freestyle session where he would just rap about whatever he saw out in the crowd.

I had been in a dark place, so I chose a song of lament. The lyrics were real, not some fake song I scribbled just for the conference. It mentioned God, but it wasn't a Christian song. It rapped about God like Tupac often did. I edited out a bunch of curse words on the fly, and it totally connected with the crowd. Afterward, I had a handful of people waiting to talk to me. It was just like the Boys and Girls Club all over again.

I went back to my hotel room that night feeling good about my decision to come to Atlanta. But my roommates decided they wanted to have a serious conversation that night. They had figured out I wasn't a Christian and were trying to evangelize me or something. My roommate, Ray, had previously asked me if I had faith. Not wanting to give myself away, I told him I did.

"Man, I think you have faith, but not saving faith," Ray said.

I shrugged it off, but it had me shook. Really disturbed. That night, I didn't think about the seminars or the way I killed the talent show. My mind was consumed with his comment.

What is the difference between faith and saving faith anyway?

I didn't know. But I was about to find out.

★ ★ ★

The final night of the conference was New Year's Eve. All the attendees were gathering in the hotel ballroom for a message and a concert before the countdown to midnight.

I was typically late, so I had to sit in the overflow room where Pastor James White's sermon was live streaming from the main room. Something about this guy was different from other preachers I'd heard. He was talking *to* us, not *at* us. He spoke our language, using terminology that was popular at the time so we could all understand. The ancient Christian message seemed relevant to my life for the first time.

Pastor White's description of Jesus' death on the cross was almost cinematic. It was like watching *The Passion of the Christ* for the first time. Sure, I knew that Jesus had been crucified, but I was oblivious to the details. I'd never heard that Jesus was beaten into a swollen lump of flesh. I'd never heard that he was whipped with a cat o' nine tails with sharpened pieces of bone and glass that ripped the skin off his back. I'd never heard that he had to carry his own splintering cross up a hill to the place of execution.

I'd never heard that the Roman soldiers drove nails the size of railroad spikes through his wrist.

I always thought of Jesus as this fluffy lamb of a man who walked around saying, "I love you, my children. Bless you." But the man Pastor White spoke about was more complex than that.

"Sure, Jesus was sensitive, but He was also like a lot of you tough guys in the crowd," he said. "You roughnecks out there—how dare you call my Jesus a punk!"

I began stirring in my chair. The Jesus I had pictured in my mind was frail and weak and bashful. He was the kind of person who would've been eaten alive on the streets of Southeast San Diego. But the man that Pastor White was describing was both gentle and strong. He was someone I could respect and trust at the same time.

But it all came to a head when Pastor White looked down at the pages of his Bible and read 1 Corinthians 6:20: "For you were bought at a price; therefore glorify God in your body and in your spirit, which are God's."[4]

The words hit me like hurricane winds.

Wait. I was bought at a price. The price that Jesus paid was for me? The beating and whipping and nails and dying were all done for me? For me?

Scenes from my life were flashing before my eyes. The young girls I'd messed around with in secret as a child. The pain and insignificance resulting from my father's absence. The apathy I felt as a child about Big Momma's missions work. The fistfuls of paper I'd ripped from the Bible. The way I'd flippantly used God's name as a curse word. Everything I'd stolen, everything I'd smoked, everyone I'd slept with. I saw all my rebellion in a flash.

Even though He knew all my mistakes, God still died for me. I don't even like God, and God loves me. Despite everything, God bought me at a price.

My inhibitions disintegrated, and I collapsed to my knees. I'm not a crier, but tears were running down my cheeks. I didn't care anymore.

"Please forgive me, God. I'm so sorry. Please forgive me. I'm so sorry."

Pastor White led us in a prayer, and I prayed like I had never prayed before. I admitted everything (as if God didn't already know the details), and I begged forgiveness for it all. When he said "Amen," I rose to my feet as if for the first time. It was like the weight I'd been carrying my whole life had been lifted. All of the baggage and all of the depression and all of the pent-up anger had been released. It felt like someone had cleaned the filthiest and ugliest parts of me—parts that even I was too ashamed to deal with.

Before that night, I wasn't sure what I believed, but now I knew. God created this world. God was working through history. God sent Jesus to earth. Jesus died for me. The Bible was true, this Jesus thing was true, it was all true. Maybe this was the rescue I'd been hoping for. Maybe God was the father I'd been wanting. He had chosen me, and I had been bought at a price.

★ ★ ★

The sermon was followed by a Cross Movement concert, but I heard their music with new ears. All the lyrics that sounded strange before now made sense. It was like these songs were written for me, like they were the soundtrack for my new life. I let myself go, partying and jumping with everybody else. After the concert, we all counted down to midnight.

3-2-1 . . . "Happy New Year!"

But this moment marked more than the start of a new year for me. It was a new era—the first day of the rest of my life.

I didn't need to smoke weed anymore; this moment felt better than being high.

I didn't need to sleep with random women anymore; I knew God had something more fulfilling for me.

I didn't need to impress people with stupid behavior anymore; I was now part of a community that valued humility over ego.

I didn't need to keep trying to fill the hole left by my absent dad; I had gained a heavenly Father.

For the first time in my life, I felt a sense of purpose and identity.

When the cheers died down, I needed to spend some time processing the significant spiritual experience I'd just had. Since I wasn't very close to anyone at the conference, I decided to find a quiet place where I could be alone with God. I walked through the hotel lobby, jumped on the elevator, and hit the button for the top floor. If I was going to talk to God, I figured I should get as high up as possible so we could hear each other clearly.

The elevator opened to a rooftop pavilion, and I stepped into the night. The city of Atlanta stretched out in front of me. Lights shone through skyscraper windows, and cars sped down the streets below. Beyond the city was an expanse of trees that faded into the darkness.

FOR THE FIRST TIME IN MY LIFE, I FELT A SENSE OF PURPOSE AND IDENTITY.

So you made all of this, huh, God? I thought.

I couldn't believe the peace I felt. Prayers just started coming out of me. I was trying to express joy and gratitude and all kinds of emotion. It didn't make much sense, but I figured God could sort it all out. I asked God all kinds of questions and then waited for an answer.

Above me was nothing but silence, but a noise began to rise from down below. A crowd of college students was chanting: "Jeeeee-sus! Jeeeee-sus! Jeeeee-sus!"

Over and over, they shouted Jesus' name. The words rose from the street and echoed on the rooftop where I stood. I can't say for sure, but it seemed to be more than a coincidence. I took it as a response from God, a welcome to the family, a sign that everything I had just experienced had been real.

It was like the God of the universe had looked down on that dark rooftop in Atlanta and spoke to His son, Lecrae, saying, "You have the answer to all of your questions . . . The answer is Jesus."

6 -
WHO AM I
FOOLIN'?

Father, I'm prayin' for a friend, he and I are pretty close,
and out of all my friends for this one I'm concerned the most.
He say he readin' daily but he ain't really learnin'.
He been in church but say that he ain't moved by any sermon.
His face weak, he ain't prayed in a week,
he wake up and just weep with his face in the sink
Lord, you gotta help my man, I'm prayin' for him daily
. . . God I know it's killin' You because it's killin' me
and matter of fact there's somethin' else he's concealin' see,
the person that I've been prayin' about is really me

Lecrae | "Prayin' For You" | *After the Music Stops*

I had finally been set free, but I was about to find out if I could live free. A person can be removed from slavery in an instant, but it takes a lifetime for slavery to be removed from a person.

The first thing I did when I returned to college after my conversion was steal a Bible. It was sitting in a local church's "lost and found" box—someone else had *lost* it, but I *found* it before they did. I would often steal Bibles, devotional books, and Christian music from local bookstores, which didn't seem wrong to me at the time since I needed them to grow in my faith. I was broke, but I knew how to steal. Old habits die hard, I guess.

Regardless, these tools propelled me in what became a relentless pursuit of God. Everywhere Christians gathered, I would show up. I might be at a Methodist church on Sunday and a Pentecostal church on Wednesday. I started meeting with a student ministry leader, Dhati, twice a week in the morning to study the Bible and reflect about what God was showing me. I didn't know the doctrinal differences between denominations; I just showed up anywhere I thought I could learn more about God.

> **I HAD FINALLY BEEN SET FREE, BUT I WAS ABOUT TO FIND OUT IF I COULD LIVE FREE. A PERSON CAN BE REMOVED FROM SLAVERY IN AN INSTANT, BUT IT TAKES A LIFETIME FOR SLAVERY TO BE REMOVED FROM A PERSON.**

I started reading books by Christian authors in my spare time. Apologetics books like Josh McDowell's *More Than a Carpenter* helped me explore answers to the many difficult questions I had about faith. Another book from the Navigator's ministry taught me a system for memorizing Scripture. I scribbled memory verses on a stack of index cards and placed them on a key ring. I wore the cards around my neck so I could review them everywhere I went. When my mom saw me wearing these cards, she thought I had joined a cult. I told her that, in the lingo of my new community, I was just "on fire," but that didn't make her feel better.

I wondered where dinosaurs came from and whether they made it onto Noah's ark. I couldn't figure out how to reconcile a good and powerful God with the existence of evil in the world. I continued wrestling with the big questions of life.

People who were raised in church often talk about coming home from a summer youth camp or church revival and being on a "high." Maybe that's the best way to describe what I felt too. It felt like a high, except I didn't have to smoke any weed to experience it.

I felt satisfied from having discovered what I'd searched for most of my life. The meaning and purpose I'd wanted was there now, and the worry that used to consume me was gone. Joy replaced anxiety, and I found a new energy for learning and growing. I had found the truth about life and God and myself. I was nineteen years behind and needed to catch up.

But there are two big problems with being on a spiritual high. First, it can often lead to legalism. You want to prove—to God and your friends and even yourself—how "holy" you've become, so you make extreme modifications to your behavior. You don't want to leave doubts in anyone's mind that you're really a changed person, that you're really "on fire," that you're really "sold out." So rather than rest in God's grace, you busy yourself trying to prove your own righteousness.

Shortly after returning to campus, my theater program cast me in a play called *Women and Wallace*. The play was about a man named Wallace who was torn between eight different women. The script called for the main character to lock lips with each of them, and sure enough, I scored the lead part. I was convinced that God wouldn't want me kissing eight girls I didn't know—even as a character in a play—so I dropped out of the theater program altogether. When I left the program, I lost the scholarship that came with it.

There were obvious vices that everyone agreed weren't good: no getting drunk, no smoking weed, no sex with girls. But that soon broadened to no parties at all—except "Praise Parties," of course—and not going anywhere that would make it appear like I was getting into trouble. As someone told me, I needed to "flee even the appearance of evil." I took out my earrings, and only hung out with Christian friends.

I felt guilty whenever I had fun with something that wasn't associated with sports or church. If I slept late and missed my early morning "quiet time," I would feel less righteous the rest of the day. It was like I was trying to earn my place on the "Christian team" by outworking everybody else. The more good things I did, or bad things I avoided, the better I felt about myself.

Most of the decisions were easy to make. The pain of sacrifice was usually outweighed by the sense of satisfaction with myself. But I almost broke down when it came to the music.

At the time, "Christian music" was on the rise and "secular music" of any kind was seen as sinful by a lot of Christians. All the other serious Christians on campus assumed that when you became a Christian, you would throw all of your "secular music" away. I don't remember who the first person was to tell me I needed to do this, but I do remember that sinking feeling. I had built a CD collection for years, and it was my pride and joy. I could sit and listen to music for hours and never grow tired of it because I had so many great albums from great artists: Nas, Outkast, Lil Wayne, Eminem. I loved my music, but if that's what God required from me, who was I to say no?

One by one, I removed them from their cases until there was a pile of holographic discs on the floor. I placed them all into a trash bag and carried them to the dumpster. When the lid slammed shut, I felt sad but also proud of myself for expressing such devotion. Because I wanted

everyone else to know that I had made the ultimate sacrifice for God, I taped all the CD cases into a five-foot-tall
pillar. When my Christian friends would visit my dorm
room, I'd point to it: "Yeah, man. I had the best 'secular
music,' but, you know, I got rid of them all." It was like
Christian bragging rights. Or even worse, a monument to
my own self-righteousness.

My music began to morph during this season too.
Faith flowed into my songs and saturated the lyrics. I was
no longer talking about God like Tupac did; now I was
full-on talking about Jesus and the Bible. I felt like this
gave my music depth, but it also gave me a place to process
my own thinking.

Many days, I'd skip class and go to the school's music
lab instead to make beats and record songs. During this
phase of life, I even recorded my first song called "Krunk
for Christ." (I know, I know. But at the time, I thought it
sounded cool.) Somehow, inserting explicit theology into
my music made me feel like God was more proud of my
songs. And I was too.

But in addition to the potential for legalism, there is
another problem with spiritual highs—like all highs, they
are temporary. Eventually, you sober up. And that's when
you find out what you're really made of.

★ ★ ★

I stayed on my spiritual high for a couple of months, but
my life started fraying as I took my decision public. Dhati
asked a handful of us who had become Christians to write
out our testimonies. My testimony was printed on the
back of a pamphlet; the other side had an invitation to

Bible study on it. Now everywhere I went, I acted like a door-to-door salesperson: "What's up, man? My name is Lecrae. Check out this flyer with my testimony on it. Want to come with me to Bible study?" It was an aggressive strategy for sure, but I had nothing to lose. I didn't have any real social capital since I wasn't fully part of any group on campus.

I was so naïve that I figured when I handed this pamphlet to people, they would just automatically want to become a Christian too. *Didn't they want meaning and purpose and acceptance?* Seemed like a no-brainer to me. But it turned out to be a more difficult sell.

I'll never forget the response I got from one of my friends on campus when I handed him a pamphlet for the first time. He read it, looked up confused, and then said, "Wait. You mean you're never going to smoke weed again? You're going to stop getting drunk at parties and stuff? You're never going to sleep with girls again until you get married?"

"No, I'm not," I responded.

"You're crazy, man," he said, laughing. "This won't last."

He was right. It wouldn't last. Before long, I was bored on weekends with nowhere to go. I didn't think Christians should pick up girls or go to parties. The pressure from feeling like I was missing out was strong, and the "Christian game nights" weren't sustaining me anymore. A person can stand only so much Monopoly.

One night when I felt particularly bored and low, my buddy, Money, who had transferred to the school recently, called me. He had a nice car, played sports, and had good luck with women. He asked me to come kick it with him.

I thought I was supposed to turn him down, but something inside me took over. I agreed.

It turned out to be a serious party. Within moments of walking through the door, I gave in. One drink, then two, then two more. Before I knew it, I was drunk and grinding with girls on the dance floor and cutting up with my boys. That night, I didn't think about my views or my values or what I assumed made me a good Christian. I just let go and had fun.

The next night I went to Bible study and pretended nothing had happened. And this began an ugly cycle of living two separate lives. With my Christian friends, I was "Legalistic Lecrae"—a guy who stayed on God's good side by passing out pamphlets, coordinating Praise Parties, and staying out of trouble. With my other friends, I was "Life of the Party Lecrae"—a guy who liked to party, get drunk, and mess around with girls. The first person had a five-foot tower of secular music CD cases to prove how committed he was to Jesus; the second person would sneak off and listen to all those same artists and not tell anyone about it. In a blink, I could transform from one version of myself to the other.

After a crazy night, I'd wake up with drool crust on my mouth and a pounding headache: "Did I blow it last night? Am I still on God's good side?" I'd feel guilty and "recommit" myself to God. For the next two weeks, I'd stay out of trouble until my friends started pushing and prodding again, and then I'd break.

The summer had its way with me because I didn't have my Bible study friends back home. There was no church I was really committed to near my mom's house. I went to a couple, but they felt weirdly religious to me. If you wanted to be a good Christian teenager in these churches, it meant wearing suits and shouting and acting like a mini-deacon or mini-bishop or something. So instead, I connected spiritually elsewhere. I listened to Lauryn Hill and Erykah Badu and Common. I went to poetry slams and cyphers and grew my hair into dreads. I was all by myself at nineteen years old, and the club was calling.

I had not technically slept with a girl since I had returned from Atlanta, though "technically" doesn't mean I was treating girls right or had a real sense of boundaries. Regardless, during this summer I slept with a girl for the first time since I returned from Atlanta, and I was crushed. I felt like I had failed God and was a failure as a Christian. So I decided to quit trying. But the harder I partied and the more I ran from God that summer, the more empty my life felt.

97

When school started again, I started hanging out with this girl, Portia, who said she was a Christian. That was cool, except, like me, she didn't know how to be a Christian either. Misery loves company, and rebellion does too. We started dating and sleeping together. She basically moved into my dorm room and would get high with me, but we'd still go to church together and read the Bible together. Eventually, the partying started replacing the spiritual stuff.

My personalities really split, which sent me into the same state of depression I thought Jesus had freed me from forever. As I learned, the only thing worse than being unhappy is being unhappy right after you think you've found the secret to joy. One dark day, I was smoking weed in my car and Dhati walked up.

"Yo, what's up man," he said. "I haven't seen you in Bible study lately."

"Yeah, man, look, I'm trying to get it together," I said, holding the joint below the window so he couldn't see it.

We talked for a minute, and he left with a look of disappointment in his eyes that punched me in the gut. That's when it hit me.

"I thought my life was supposed to be great with Jesus, but it isn't. I'm sick of hiding and being two different people."

I decided to transfer to a music college in Tennessee where I could start fresh. But things did not improve there. In fact, they got worse. So I quit that school too. Within months, the teenage Lecrae who began college with a full scholarship was on his way to becoming a dropout. But back home, I got into more trouble than I ever did before.

★ ★ ★

After I moved back to Texas, I had to figure out how to make money. So my friend Ed and I hatched a scheme to throw parties for high school kids. They seemed like an easy market because they couldn't get into bars or clubs, but plenty of them wanted to party. We would host parties at hotels and random venues with live music. We'd charge kids five or ten bucks a head to get in and then sell them drinks or weed or whatever they wanted. It was a quick hustle, and I was good at it.

In order to get the word out, we would go to high schools and pass out flyers. Looking back, a twenty-one-year-old breaking into a high school campus to pretend to be a student wasn't the smartest idea, but it made sense at the time. One day I was passing out flyers at a school, and I felt that I was being watched. Out of the corner of my eye, I saw a police officer walking toward me. I turned and bolted outside, but when the doors swung open, there were cop cars everywhere. I was trespassing at a public school, which is a serious offense.

Next thing I know, my arms are pulled behind my back and I can feel the cold steel cuffs clink around my wrists. The officers begin searching my car while I sat sweating and nervous in the back of a cruiser. I knew this was going to be bad because, in addition to trespassing, I had a sack of weed in my car in plain view. I could see that one of the officers found something, and he began deliberating with the others. Finally, the officer walked over to question me about the finding.

99

"Sir, we have found something in the back of your car," he said.

"Oh yeah, what's that?" I replied.

"Whose Bible is this?" he said, holding out a nearly forgotten book I had carried to more Bible studies and church services than I could count.

"It's mine," I said.

The tattered pages were highlighted, marked up, underlined, and had notes sticking out. It was clear that its owner used it for more than a doorstop.

"You're the one who has been reading this Bible like that?" he asked.

"I need to be," I said.

He looked me up and down and then spoke: "Here's what I'm going to do for you. I'm going to let you go, but I don't want to see you here again. I don't want to find out that you've been causing trouble. Instead, I want you to get back into this Bible."

I nodded my head, and he let me go.

There are moments in life when God tries to get our attention. Moses met God in a flaming bush, Samuel heard a voice in the night, and the apostle Paul had his famous Damascus Road experience. In modern times, God often speaks in less dramatic, but equally significant, ways. The thing that matters most in moments like these is whether we are willing to listen to and heed what God is trying to say.

I'd like to say I called off the party for that week and turned over a new leaf. But that isn't true. The situation left me speechless for a few hours, and then I was back at it. We still hosted the party that weekend, and nearly two hundred kids attended. We hosted more, and attendance grew as word spread. Soon we were having four or five hundred or more at each party. Ed and I were each clearing $3,000 per night easy, which was not bad for a twenty-one-year-old without a college degree.

THE THING THAT MATTERS MOST IN MOMENTS LIKE THESE IS WHETHER WE ARE WILLING TO LISTEN TO AND HEED WHAT GOD IS TRYING TO SAY.

Over time, our parties grew famous. So famous, in fact, that MTV decided they wanted to film one. They were doing some series on underage kids who party or something, and we figured it would be cool to have one of our hotel parties on there. The only problem is that this night turned out to be absolutely crazy. Some kids were drinking

WHO AM I FOOLIN'?

huge amounts and throwing up. Others were having sex on the dance floor. A fight broke out and got out of hand. It was total chaos, and somewhere in the middle of it all, someone smashed in my friend's car windows and stole the thousands of dollars that Ed and I had made.

We were back at square one. Or square zero, really. We were broke.

I remember the emptiness I felt when I tried to sleep that night. So much time had passed since Atlanta. Since that night I met God in the hotel ballroom. Since I cried out for God to forgive me. Since I heard the voices chanting "Jesus" from the rooftop. It had been so long since I felt free like that. That night and so many before, I felt like a spiritual failure and a spiritual fraud. But I felt like God was still with me. I was making a mountain of mistakes, but I was not alone. God had seen my many failures, but He hadn't left me as a result.

101

And yet I was still unwilling to surrender. To let go. To give up control. I still wanted to run the show and carve my own path and make my own way. I wanted God in my life, but only in the background. I wasn't giving up the starring role. Somehow I ignored the fact that whenever I took the lead, I always messed things up. Little did I know, I was about to mess things up again by making the greatest mistake of my life.

★ ★ ★

Now that I was penniless, I decided to start looking for a steady paying job. In the local job listings, I found an entry from a call center and, even though I'd never done anything like that, assumed it was better than nothing. My girlfriend at the time—we'll call her "Kim"—applied too, and we both got jobs.

The attraction between Kim and me was electric. She was smart and beautiful, loved music and liked to sing, was artistic and adventurous. And she liked to get high as much as I did. We started having sex immediately, and one time we didn't use protection. But since we smoked a lot of weed together, and I was under the impression that marijuana made people sterile, I figured we had nothing to worry about. I couldn't have been more wrong.

One day Kim and I walked out behind the call center during a smoke break but she didn't want a cigarette.

With a nervous look in her eyes, she confessed: "I think I'm pregnant."

Not wanting to wait, I took Kim to the store on our lunch break that day for a pregnancy test. Sure enough, it came back positive. I made her take two more tests, but the results were the same. My mind raced.

This can't happen right now. I don't have a college degree, and I'm living paycheck to paycheck in some stupid telemarketing job. All I do all day is smoke weed and make beats. How am I going to take care of a baby? Things are bad enough as it is. I can't let some kid ruin my situation.

In the face of significant choices, people tend to weigh the options and determine which course will cause them less pain. All the evidence in my selfish young mind fell into the "this is going to jack up my life" column. A baby meant obligations, financial burdens, the end of freedom and fun. Because I was too afraid to tell anyone else, no one reminded me that children are a gift from God or that family could help lift the burdens or that a decision to abort my child would have lifelong psychological effects.

The weight of the decision caused nightmares. Shame haunted me in my sleep. I knew I was running from God.

When I woke up, I would have to numb the conviction by getting drunk or high to rest. The panic built over the next couple of days until one afternoon the dam broke. I jumped into my car and sped to Kim's house.

"Yo, this can't happen," I said. "It just can't. It is going to mess up everything for both of us."

Kim said she was torn. She recognized that her life was a mess, but part of her felt like she should have the baby.

"You need to let go of that thought, Kim," I told her. "This isn't even a conversation."

Your true character is revealed not by how you act when life goes your way, but how you act when the bottom falls out. Though I didn't realize it, my behavior was telling how broken I was. Kim was devastated and desperate, but I remained firm. I gave her only one option: go to the doctor, get rid of this thing, and let's move forward with our lives.

She loved me and trusted me. I was a little older, persistent, and persuasive. I rarely lost an argument with her. I could tell she didn't want to get rid of the baby, but I was determined to wear her down.

YOUR TRUE CHARACTER IS REVEALED NOT BY HOW YOU ACT WHEN LIFE GOES YOUR WAY, BUT HOW YOU ACT WHEN THE BOTTOM FALLS OUT.

Once she was persuaded, I left her for a few hours to gather all the money I had and borrow some extra from a friend. I returned, put her in my car, and drove straight to the nearest family planning clinic in our depressed neighborhood in East Dallas.

The gray medical building wasn't a pristine, welcoming place. Not by a long shot. It was old and cold. The parking lot was full of potholes, and it was located just down the block from a liquor store and a check-cashing place. I walked Kim inside and helped her fill out the paperwork. We sat silent in the waiting room until they called her name. She looked at me, and I stood up. She followed my lead and went with the nurse into the procedure room. I told her I was going to drive around until it was over, and I left.

I was mostly relieved. The implications of what we were doing were not very clear to me at the time. I was glad that I didn't have to tell our parents and glad that my future plans—whatever they were—weren't interrupted.

I prayed and told God that I knew I was wrong and I was going to change after all of this.

More than an hour later, a nurse rolled Kim outside in a wheelchair. She had a blank expression on her face from all of the pain medication. I helped her into my car, drove her home, snuck her past her mom, and put her to bed. When I left, I could tell she was still jacked up from the medication, but she also was depressed. In my rush to escape the situation, I had convinced her to do something she didn't really want to do.

WHEN PEOPLE TRY TO AVOID SUFFERING BY SINNING, THEY END UP SINNING THEIR WAY INTO SUFFERING.

On my ride home, I refused to let myself feel guilty. I worked hard to convince myself that it was an acceptable decision, even though deep down I knew it was wrong. I had sacrificed my baby's life so I could keep my options open. But when people try to avoid suffering by sinning, they end up sinning their way into suffering. And this was exactly what happened in my life.

I was pretty callous. It was yet another wound I'd tuck away like the rest. I buried this skeleton like I'd done so many times before. I was becoming numb to the greater meaning behind my actions.

After that day, Kim's depression worsened. It became clear she wasn't going to snap out of it, and I told her it wasn't working for me any longer. I don't remember what I said to her the day we broke up, but I probably threw in something spiritual about us both needing to get right with God or whatever. I was feeding her a line that I didn't believe, but it may have been the truest thing I'd ever said to her.

My life was spiraling out of control. And I had to hit rock bottom before I could realize I needed to rise up.

7 -
WELCOME
TO REHAB

Check me in
I know I'm sick and my addiction got me itchin',
Everyday I need a fixin',
I ain't quittin til it kill me . . .
Euphoria come and go but it's something you can't grasp
Yeah, we're grasping for the emptiness,
Hoping we can catch . . . something

Lecrae | "Check In" | *Rehab*

When I arrived on the North Texas campus the first time, smoking weed was one of my biggest vices. But when I returned to try to finish my education, it might have been the least of them. To cope with the abortion, I'd moved on to cocaine and ecstasy.

I was drinking constantly and often driving drunk. One night after getting fired from my job, I was drinking and driving and ended up flipping my car four times. My car was totaled, but somehow I walked away intact. On the outside at least. I was a wreck on the inside.

The slightest offense would have me in a drunken rage, and the fights I was getting into were serious. There were times when some people even pulled out knives and guns. One time my friends and I stomped a dude's head into the ground after he accused my buddy of flirting with his girl. You know you've lost your grip on reality when you try to fight an entire football team. (That didn't end well for me, or my left eye.) It was like I was finally able to express all the wrath I'd stored up for years but didn't know was there.

Returning as an upperclassman, I finally had some clout on campus. I was getting invited to the best parties and had way more social capital with everybody, including beautiful women. I was running through them left and right. Some weeks, I'd sleep with a different girl almost every night.

I was a tornado of rage, confusion, and hormones ripping through Denton, Texas, and I was on the verge of destroying myself. I was headed for rock bottom before, but I now had finally arrived. I didn't know who I was, and the guilt from abandoning the God I'd met in Atlanta was gnawing at me from inside. I prayed that God would intervene and force me to change, and when He didn't I'd end up depressed.

What would become of Lecrae Moore? I'd tried everything—even Jesus—but nothing stuck. I had already made it further in life than most of the men who helped raise me, so I had no vision for a better future. My identity was wrapped up in people's perception of me, and that fluctuated almost as often as my mood swings. One night, at my lowest point, I decided it was time to push the ejection button. I wasn't doing the world any more favors than the world was doing me.

I raided my fridge, guzzling all the alcohol my stomach could hold. I swallowed all the pills in my cabinet—painkillers and cold medicine and even some anti-depression meds that a counselor had given me. I tossed them back, and as they fell down my throat, I thought, *I hope I die.*

Stumbling and dizzy, I ended up on my back staring up at the moving ceiling. God will let me into heaven, right? I mean, I am a Christian even if I don't always act like it. I wonder what heaven will be like? It has to be better than the hell of my current existence.

My eyes closed.

Hours passed.

Surprisingly, I woke up in the same spot where I'd laid down.

★ ★ ★

Everything came to a head one night when my biggest vices—substance abuse, women, and rage—collided.

The music thumped at the party I was at, and it was getting late. I'd been flirting with a girl all night, but she had a boyfriend. But since I was drunk out of my mind, my judgment was even worse than normal. When she was on a call with her boyfriend, I snatched the phone and started taunting him, and he got heated. I challenged him to do something about it, but I was joking. He didn't catch the humor. Things got heated between us, and later on he showed up at the party raving mad and looking for me.

I had already left, but word got back to me that he had a gun. I could hear my Uncle Chris's voice in my head: "Don't be a punk. Stand up for yourself."

I had been holding onto my sanity by a frayed strand, but in that moment something snapped and I lost control. I was embarrassed and afraid I'd look weak if I let it ride. Rage boiled up inside me, and before I knew what happened I was in my car. I was headed to my mom's house to get her gun, come back to school, and make this guy pay. The fury was consuming me, and it was like I had lost control of my body. Looking back, I'm not sure where it came from. Maybe it was all of the rage from childhood and adolescence that I had accumulated and stuffed away. The disappointments. The abandonment. The loneliness. I'd never really dealt with the pain, but I felt it now. I was looking for vengeance.

With my headlights cutting the darkness ahead and the alcohol still circulating in my veins, my foot pressed the gas pedal further toward the floor. Sixty miles per hour, then seventy, then eighty. I was driving out of control, weaving in and out of lanes and around cars.

A shouting match broke out inside of me as I tried to decide what I should do. It was like one of those cartoons where there is an angel on one shoulder and a devil on the other.

"What are you doing, man? Who cares about this dude?" I asked.

"I care. I can't just let someone threaten me with a gun. I can't just do nothing," I replied.

"What do you think you're going to do that is going to change anything?" I said. "Just let it go."

"Let it go?" I replied. "Nope. I'm going to kill him."

"Well you're going to end up in jail. You're going to ruin your life!"

"My life is already ruined. There is no point in me living anyway."

I was a living picture of the apostle James's words: "A double minded man is unstable in all his ways."[5] Hands shaking and mind racing, my thoughts grew darker. I was even considering steering my car into oncoming traffic just to commit suicide. The voice of reason was losing, and the devil on my shoulder was winning the fight.

And then it happened.

"Pull over, Lecrae! There's a hospital right there!" a third voice inside shouted. "Go into the hospital and tell them you're going to hurt someone!"

In a moment that I can't really explain, my hands jerked the wheel of the car to the side. The tires screeched as I flew into the parking lot and skidded to a stop. I rushed from the car into the emergency room and stared the receptionist in the eyes: "I'm about to kill somebody or kill myself. Y'all better do something."

In a matter of minutes, a police officer was bending my arms behind my back and placing cuffs around my wrist. They questioned me, and when it was clear to them I was a danger to myself and others, they decided to take me to a facility that could help me.

There was no going back now. I was on my way to rehab.

★ ★ ★

I was numb riding in the police car to Timberlawn Psychiatric Center. I didn't realize I was depressed; I just knew I was jacked up. Like Leonardo DiCaprio in *The Departed*, I was cold and stark and not vulnerable. I was cut off from my emotions, but I wanted to reconnect. I just didn't know how.

The electric doors at the entrance to Timberlawn parted like the Red Sea. Unlike the Israelites, however, I was headed *into* captivity. It was not a welcoming place—not even a greeter to meet you at the door. It was one of the largest mental health and rehab facilities in East Dallas, and ironically, just a few miles from the abortion clinic I'd taken Kim to less than a year before.

I remember some of the check-in process, but only in flashes. Sitting in the waiting room. Flash. *Sign this, Mr. Moore.* Flash. *We need your belt.* Flash. *And shoelaces.* Flash. *Put these clothes on.* Flash. *Please follow me.* After a brief psychological evaluation, I was led to my room.

The metal door had a little glass window in it—my only connection to other people. I was completely cut off now. All alone to think about my life and the mess I'd made of it. Sitting on the edge of my bed and staring at the floor, I felt a longing to let go. To let go of the effort. Let go of the frustration. Let go of the anger. Let go of the steering wheel of my life. I was willing to take whatever advice or prescription could help me.

Despair turned to boredom. My room was as lifeless and empty as I felt. White walls, a bed, a desk. If I wasn't going crazy when I walked in here, this place would drive me crazy before I left. Soon, the attendant opened my door and told me my mom had come to visit, and my stomach dropped. In much of the black community, going to rehab is considered shameful. I know of people whose family noticed they needed help, but rather than check them into a professional facility they would "rehabilitate" them by driving them miles outside of the city to let them throw up and sleep in the car for a few days. If a kid goes to rehab, a mom in a black neighborhood might even hide it from the rest of her family. That's why rehab is seldom talked about, even though people sometimes go there.

My mom had gotten out of the hood and made something of herself. She had escaped the mentality that often leads to multiple pregnancies and baby daddies. She had helped me get into college. She was determined to make sure her kids didn't end up in jail or on the streets or in rehab. But here I was.

And I see her face coming through the little glass hole, and the door opened and she saw me. I'm in my uniform looking all pitiful and—POW—it hits her. A wave of shame and sadness. She was crushed and began to wail.

"Ma, it's not your fault," I said. "I did this. It's my fault. But don't worry. I'm getting out of here, and I'm going to get things right."

Few things are worse than seeing your own mother break down in tears and knowing you were the cause of it. I'd never seen my mom cry except maybe once during my entire life. I didn't know how to stop her crying. I only knew that I had caused it. Standing before a mother who loved me that I had put through the ringer for more than two decades was a moment of bigness and brokenness. Her tears became wrecking balls. They were tearing down my walls as I realized the gravity of my situation.

I didn't cry with her. I couldn't. I've never been an outwardly sensitive person. I would only let out my emotions when I was alone or writing music or poetry. My grandfather was likely in the CIA, and he died alone in his apartment having rarely told anyone he loved them. I never met him, but from the stories I've heard I always felt like he and I were cut from the same cloth. But even though my eyes were dry, I felt like I was crying on the inside.

I had always been afraid of being weak as a child, but that's exactly what I had become. Weak. But as it turns out, moments of weakness are opportunities for God to show Himself strong. I knew it was time to let go. I just needed to figure out how.

★ ★ ★

My days in rehab cycled between group counseling and isolation. Being with a group was almost an out-of-body experience. I went into observer mode and remained mostly quiet. You didn't have to share unless you wanted to, but even if they had made me, I wouldn't have known what to say. The thought running through my mind was, "I'm not like these people." They were all seriously messed up.

MOMENTS OF WEAKNESS ARE OPPORTUNITIES FOR GOD TO SHOW HIMSELF STRONG.

114

In my first session, I remember sitting across from someone who drank a gallon of Jack Daniels a day. There was a girl who was strung out on drugs because her father kept raping her. Listening to them tell their stories, I realized that I was the only one in the facility who was a college student. The only one who had been given a range of opportunities to break the cycle and succeed. But I had squandered all of them.

When I wasn't in group counseling, I was stuck in the solitude of my room. Being forced to sit in an empty room, cut off from the world, was awful. But it turned out to be exactly what I needed. For the first time in my life, I was able to process everything I'd experienced without distractions or peer pressure. I didn't have to live up to anyone else's standard in that room. I could just think. There was only one item in my room to keep me busy. I noticed a small book sitting on top of the desk. Leather-bound and familiar, it was a Gideon Bible like you often find in hotel rooms.

I picked it up and turned to the book of Romans. I started reading and couldn't stop. Chapter after chapter, it was like the words had been written for me.

"You also are among those Gentiles who are called to belong to Jesus Christ."[6]

"Professing to be wise, they became fools."[7]

"For even though they knew God, they did not honor Him as God or give thanks."[8]

"To those who are selfishly ambitious and do not obey the truth, but obey unrighteousness, wrath and indignation. There will be tribulation and distress. . . ."[9]

I kept reading because it was really speaking to me. And then I came to the sixth chapter:

> *What benefit did you reap at that time from the things you are now ashamed of? Those things result in death! But now that you have been set free from sin and have become slaves of God, the benefit you reap leads to holiness, and the result is eternal life. For the wages of sin is death, but the gift of God is eternal life in Christ Jesus our Lord.*[10]

It was like a blindfold fell off my eyes. I'd been celebrating things I should have been ashamed of, and I had
been ashamed of what I should have been celebrating. I
had been set free, but I was still living like a slave to my
old life and old habits and old ways. I'd been liberated
from slavery, but slavery had not been liberated from me.
I saw Jesus as my Savior, but not my Lord. I thought that
because God had given me grace, I could just do whatever
I wanted. But doing whatever I pleased was only going to
bring death. Surrendering to God was the key to receiving
life.

I walked back to the door and knocked until an
attendant came. They mentioned during check-in that
one of the few things you were allowed to do in your
room was draw. So I asked for paper and something to
write with. Since a pencil or pen was a potential danger
to patients, they offered me a crayon. I had been going
hard for months, but rehab gave me hours to sit alone with
God. With a Bible in one hand and a crayon in the other,
I began reading the Word and writing down everything
God was saying. And He was teaching me mind-blowing
things that no one else had ever told me.

★ ★ ★

When I decided to follow Jesus that night in Atlanta, I
assumed that becoming a Christian would make life easier.
I thought the rest of my life would be smiling and smooth
sailing. I assumed I wouldn't be tempted by women and
partying and acceptance and all the things that I'd been a
slave to for so many years. I thought I would walk around

with a continual inner peace and serenity like Gandhi or something.

This turns out to be a lie that too many people believe. You'll actually experience *more* temptation, not *less*, after you become a Christian. Following Jesus doesn't mean you'll start living perfectly overnight. It certainly doesn't mean that your problems will disappear. Rather than ridding you of problems or temptations, following Jesus just means that you have a place—no, a person—to run to when they come. And the power to overcome them.

I wish someone had told me this after that night in Atlanta. Because when I started stumbling and faltering after I became a Christian, I hid my struggles. Why? Because I didn't think it was supposed to go down like that. And because too many Christians I know lived by the same lie and condemned, shamed, and rejected other Christians who messed up. Since I thought I was supposed to be instantly sinless and my Christian friends did too, I lived a double life. I acted like a Christian around other Christians, but I let loose whenever I wasn't.

I can't tell you where we got the idea that following Jesus is some kind of quick fix for all of our struggles, but it wasn't from the Bible. No, the Scripture is like one big, unbroken story about people who decided to follow God and ended up failing almost as much as they succeeded.

After God told Abraham that he was going to have millions of kids, the old man literally laughed in God's face. Jacob was a lying cheat before he met God at Bethel. And he was a lying cheat afterward too. These are two of Israel's greatest patriarchs. Moses was a murderer, a doubter, an excuse-maker. He was chosen to lead God's people out of slavery. David was "a man after God's own heart." But he was also an adulterer. His son, Solomon, was the wisest man who ever lived. But he had hundreds of wives. And Jesus' disciples were all flawed in their own way—from Thomas, the doubter, to Peter, the hothead. With such a long list of people who both followed God and stumbled constantly, why would we assume our experiences would be any different?

But somehow we do.

We fool ourselves into thinking that when we're "born again" we come out of the womb walking. But spiritual infants are like physical infants. When a child begins to learn how to walk, they fall a lot. I remember when my oldest son took his first step. My wife and I were so excited, but we *expected* him to fall right after he took it. And he did. But we didn't condemn him for stumbling. We were patient and encouraging. We clapped when he got back up and cheered him on for continuing to try.

WE FOOL OURSELVES INTO THINKING THAT WHEN WE'RE "BORN AGAIN" WE COME OUT OF THE WOMB WALKING.

Each time he attempted to walk, he would take more steps than the last time. But he would still fall, and sometimes he hurt himself. By letting him fail and loving him through it, he eventually succeeded. Now walking is a way of life for him. He can even run a race.

As with children, there is no time period for figuring out how to walk. Some kids are quick learners, and others take their time. This is also true spiritually. After the Apostle Paul was converted, he retreated to the desert for three years and came back in full force. But it took Moses forty years in the desert to get his act together. Because God is a perfect parent, He is patient with us whether we are more like the forty-year-old Moses or the three-year-old Paul. We need to have the same patience with each other and with ourselves as we make our way out of our deserts.

Nov. 14, 2011 — AMSTERDAM, Holland

TODAY is what I hope to be the beginning of a new season. One where I am intensely hungry for God & H.S Holy word, Hungry for Relationship. I'm headed to Africa with my labelmates and excited to spread the fame of Christ mostly excited to have time to sit still reflect, Grow + PRAY. None of which I have done in so long. The money, fame, opportunities I suck have flooded out the sweet quiet moments with God. Add to that 3 wonderful kids & I find myself buried without much time to myself + for God Godward intimacy. I pray this all changes. I'm so addicted to media. So addicted to hearing the worlds perspective of me & lost my burden to see a world know Jesus. (Epiphany!) That I pray changes I'm not quite sure how to navigate that artistically but I think it needs to start privately. I have to be burdened to know and want More Jesus. How can I spread a fame for someone I'm not impressed by or I'm not interested in knowing more of. God I pray my affection for You changes & I see an increased desire to see your name known. because my appitite for you Lord. I am not where I should be but you will never leave nor forsake. I lay my heart soul in your hands. Change me.

Many people don't act like this. Because we tend to only tell stories about the fast-learning ones who find walking easy, we don't tell many stories about those of us who fall. We just ignore them or condemn them or shame them. And because we don't know any stories of the many others who are falling, we assume that we are the only ones who do.

Before rehab, I was trying to walk out of the desert by my own strength. That's how I'd done everything my whole life, and no one told me that it should be any different after becoming a Christian. But now I realized that I had someone to help me learn how to walk, a parent who was patient when I stumbled and who would help teach me to walk if I'd let Him. Falling wasn't the end of the world as long as I got back up and kept walking. After all, repentance is a continual act—a lifestyle—rather than a single event.

By the time I left rehab, I'd begun to finally surrender to my own imperfections. I'd been brought low by the embarrassment of being there and my crying mother's visit. My mother was sad because I'd stumbled, but she was cheering me on to get back up. In the same way, God refused to give up on me. He was still showing up, still waiting, and still wanting to help me start again.

★ ★ ★

I was able to discharge myself from Timberlawn a week after arriving, and I couldn't sign those papers fast enough. My mom picked me up and immediately started planning the way forward with me. She was still blaming herself a little bit and wondering if this was all connected to my childhood traumas. More than anything, she was trying to figure out how to help me get my life back on track. I let her talk it out, but I already knew what I needed to do.

Since I no longer believed the lie that I could walk on my own, I knew I needed help. I moved in with my friend James. I was still paying rent at my current apartment, but I couldn't afford *not* to make the move. James would sit with me and talk to me and encourage me. When I stumbled, as I often would, I could be honest with him about it and he wouldn't bash me like some other Christians would have. Each morning, we would read the Bible together and just talk real with each other.

In addition to James, there were others. I spent more time with my friend Joe, who was also willing to get into my business and tell me the truth. "I always got your back, bro, but you need to know that you struggle with acceptance," he told me. By telling me the truth without condemning me, Joe was helping me understand how I'd been finding my identity in women and social worth and other substitutes. Joe had been going to seminary, and he started to introduce me to great Christian thinkers like C. S. Lewis who, in some way, also joined the community that was supporting me.

I WAS LEARNING TO WALK ON MY OWN AS I LEARNED TO WALK ALONGSIDE OTHERS.

Suddenly I had a group of people who were pushing me forward with encouragement and honesty and grace and truth. Nothing in my life had ever humbled me like being in rehab, and nothing in my life had ever renewed me like being in true Christian community. I was learning to walk on my own as I learned to walk alongside others.

In the front of my mind was a verse from Romans that God gave me in solitary confinement while reading that little Gideon Bible: *For I am not ashamed of the gospel, for it is the power of God for salvation to everyone who believes.*[11]

A lot of people puff up when they recite this verse like it's some sort of Christian bragging right. They think this verse is a way to declare how strong you are, how tough you are, how brave you are. But that is the opposite of what this verse means. Instead, it is a manifesto for the broken. For the needy. For the helpless. For the ones who are stumbling more than they are stepping. For the ones who are willing to admit that they aren't brave enough, tough enough, or strong enough.

I can't save myself through my own strength, through pretending. By working harder or pulling myself up by my boot straps. There's no woman that can save me. No drug that can save me. No program or clinic that can save me. I no longer thought I was a Christian because I was strong and had it all together; I now knew I was a Christian because I'm weak and admitted I need a Savior. There was no other power that could save me outside of the power of God.

All my life, I'd been hiding pieces of myself and putting up a front. I'd been hiding my weakness so everyone would think I was hard. So that people would like me. I finally let go of all that and surrendered. Now I refused to hide my struggles and imperfections, my temptations and my problems. I refused to exhaust myself trying to conform to others' expectations or fit in their boxes. For the first time in my life, I was free to live. *Unashamed.*

8 - CONFESSIONS OF A CHRISTIAN RAPPER

—

You like music from rap to gospel
But ya prolly never heard nobody rap the gospel
Different sound but the truth's the same
With no choirs no bands but the truth remains

Lecrae | "Jesus Muzik" | *After the Music Stops*

—

I had fully committed to following Jesus, but the ghost of my father's absence was still haunting me. Unknown to me at the time, being abandoned by him was impacting my faith.

I had never called anyone "Dad" my entire life, so thinking about God as my Father felt weird. As a child and teenager, I wondered if my biological father abandoned me because I wasn't good enough or worthy of love. I felt like maybe one day I could earn his respect, affection, and presence. This distorted view of what a father is like bled into the way I related to God.

My whole life I'd been craving a male role model to fill the void left by my father, and now I felt like God could be that for me. But deep down I wondered if my relationship with my heavenly Father was as fragile as my relationship with my earthly one. If I made God mad by misbehaving or not doing enough good things for Him, would He leave me too? I didn't know the answer, but I wasn't going to risk it. Every day turned into a quest to earn God's approval.

I stopped answering many of my non-Christian friends' phone calls so I wouldn't risk being negatively influenced by them. I stayed away from women so that I wouldn't accidentally stumble into a sexual relationship. And I wouldn't come within a mile of a party on campus. I would have told you that I didn't believe good works could earn me salvation, but I was living like they could.

Even the way I did evangelism became skewed. It became something of a competition for me to prove to God and others that I was worthy and committed. Instead of just trying to love non-Christians well and treat them like Jesus would, I tried to argue them into a corner where they had to convert in order to escape. Rather than focusing on winning people, I was trying to win arguments.

"What's up, man?" I might ask a stranger.

"Just chillin'."

"Let me ask you a question, man," I'd say. "Have you ever told a lie?"

"Uh, yeah."

"Have you ever stolen something? Even something small?" I'd ask.

"Yeah. Why?"

"That means you're a liar and a thief," I'd say. "You have broken two of God's commandments, man. And if you've broken any of them, God says you've broken all of them."

Getting in a stranger's face and calling him a liar isn't the most effective way to start a conversation. I didn't care about who this person was or what he might be experiencing. I wasn't interested in investing in his life or trying to help meet his needs. I just wanted to win him over so I could check another name off and move on to the next person. I was oblivious to how obnoxious I was and how poorly I treated people.

Once when I was walking into the campus library, I noticed another student in strange clothing. I walked over and struck up a conversation.

"Hey man, are you a Muslim?" I asked, extending my arm.

"Yes, I am," he replied, shaking my hand.

"Nice to meet you. My name is Lecrae. I'm a Christian, which means you just shook an infidel's hand," I said. "You aren't actually living what you believe."

The student became enraged, and we started shouting at each other in the middle of the library. He told me to get away from him, and I did, but not before I told him that he believed in a demon rather than the true God and needed to repent. I puffed up as I walked away, proud that I had earned another stripe for Jesus. I remember thinking that night how I had showed him and even imagined that he was probably at home wrestling with his beliefs because of what I had said. Looking back, I think my behavior probably made him *less* convinced that Christianity was worth considering.

As you can imagine, people didn't always respond so well to my abrasive arguments. But that didn't matter; I wore rejection like a badge of honor. If someone got angry or hurled insults at me, I could brag to my friends that I had been "persecuted" by some punk nonbeliever for the sake of the gospel. I never considered that maybe I was the silly one in this situation. One time, I was trying to evangelize someone who was standing in a line outside of a club, and they got so angry that they spit in my face. I felt like I had really suffered for the cause of Christ. It was like I was taking the machismo of the gangsta mentality and wrapping it in Christianity.

Sept 25th

Lord you are the giver of wisdom & in your hands all things are controlled.

Father please allow stores to get the cd on time still kill my hearts desire to see & know how they do sales wise. No yours will be done. Kill my pride & do not allow it to thrive. I pray for our community here that all this will lead to Biblical reform. My you increase BJ's wisdom. Humble me more. Decrease our desire to be right. Increase our desire to love you. Grow my family. Develop them & grow their hearts toward you. I pray for Cinni & our talk. I pray she'd be encouraged to seek you, & you would guide her to growth. I pray that she'd live for your glory. I pray for the See Retreat. Give me words & ways to speak life into their hearts.

The more I avoided doing "bad" things and accomplished "good" things, the more I felt loved and accepted by God. I had made the same mistake a lot of Christians make: I saw my connection with God as a *contractual* relationship, rather than a *covenantal* relationship. All contracts have terms, but covenants don't. They last forever. In a contractual relationship, you're always worried about breaking the rules. In a covenantal relationship, you're only concerned with loving the other party as much as you can.

The unresolved pain from fatherlessness had messed with my psychology.

My psychology had messed with my Christianity.

And both of them were influencing the music.

★ ★ ★

After graduating from North Texas, I got a job working for a local cable company. I had a serious and steady paycheck for the first time in my life. After spending years facing just about every kind of problem a kid could run into, I felt like my life might finally stabilize. James and my other friends kept me out of trouble most nights, and I was in church or leading Bible studies the rest of the time.

To fill my free time, I volunteered at a local juvenile detention center. The boys there had stories similar to mine: fatherlessness, substance abuse, objectification of women, no real sense of identity. And, of course, a love for hip-hop.

To pass the time and connect with them, we'd get in a circle and I'd rap just like old times in Skyline Hills and at the Boys and Girls Club and in the talent show in Atlanta.

The only difference was that the lyrics were now all about God and Jesus and faith.

The kids at the detention center began urging me to record a mixtape, but it wasn't the easiest thing to do. The technology that many amateur musicians use to record tracks today wasn't available at the time. During college, I used the school music lab to make beats; but after graduation, I was left high and dry. "Luckily," I caught a break when a friend who had studio equipment went to prison. I "borrowed" his machine while he was in jail and started recording tracks in my spare time.

Being able to record music gave me a leg up on a lot of other young musicians. But unknown to me, my songs were terrible. The recording quality was not great, and the lyrics were often cheesy. I was just happy to be able to record anything at all. Thankfully, my friend Otis had the guts to tell me what was up.

"All your songs suck, man," he said. "You need to go into a studio and create songs that sound like when you rap in circles with your friends. *That* would be dope."

Otis's words sucker-punched me, but I knew he was right. I hadn't committed to excellence, and this dose of the truth forced me to make a change.

I wrote and rewrote song after song. I was determined to be better. I worked on my production skills, often staying up until the sunrise to perfect my craft in the studio. I needed to improve, and that was going to take time.

My hard work paid off, and I got better. But I knew I couldn't get to the next level by myself. Luckily, I recently had become friends with a tall white kid from Louisiana named Ben Washer.

★ ★ ★

The first time we met, I knew he was a smart and earnest entrepreneur, with many of the business skills I lacked. Ben had moved out to Denton, Texas, to take part in a discipleship program led by a local pastor and spent the summer at an inner-city sports camp. In an effort to find music that would connect with young campers, he looked for high-quality hip-hop with a Christian worldview. Over time, he developed a golden ear.

Ben volunteered at a detention center with me, and we talked about music during down times. One day he proposed working with me to create a theme song for the next summer's camp. I had nothing to lose, so we rented some studio time and put together a track on a shoestring budget.

The song, "Crossover," caught fire at camp and spread well beyond. As it became successful, Ben caught a vision for something bigger. He realized that there was an opportunity for more good hip-hop from Christians in the marketplace and wanted to start a music label. Ben offered to make me one of its first artists if I was interested.

I deliberated for about ten seconds.

If a record label was pressing up CDs for me, I wouldn't have to spend what little money I had on it. So I agreed, and Ben and a friend of his emptied out their life savings to jumpstart the project.

Just like that, Reach Records was born.

Together, we found a way to record my first album, *Real Talk*. I bought a little purple drum and began producing. Ben bought time in random small studios and hip-hop spots around town so we could record music.

Night after night, I made beats and wrote lyrics. I'd fall asleep at work from staying up too late. I'd write rhymes at the gas station waiting for my car to fill up and at the grocery store in the middle of the cereal aisle. Soon, we began enlisting others. My roommate, Tedashii, was an incredible rapper who had done some popular freestyle sessions on campus. We enlisted him to rap on many of the songs. BJ, my best friend at the time, didn't rap at all, but we found a way to squeeze him on a track intro. Somehow, our ragtag team pieced the whole record together. It was thrilling. But once we had a product we were proud of, we needed to figure out how to sell it.

I carried boxes of CDs around to record stores and convinced a few of them to buy an album. A day or two later, I would tell all my friends the only way to get my CD was to purchase it at these particular stores. The word spread, and soon the stores couldn't keep them in stock. With the stores promoting them, people starting listening to the music.

Meanwhile, Ben was working other angles for generating buzz. He turned out to be a phenomenal salesperson—if he had been raised in Southeast San Diego, he definitely would've been a hustler—convincing people who had never heard of us to order cases of CDs. He was resourceful, even using his background in architecture and computer science to design all of our logos himself. Ben's passion to change lives through music drove him to work tirelessly to shape the vision and direction of our new record label.

Word about the music started to spread because it was rap by a Christian that sounded current. It had a Southern flavor and remained true to language of the broader hip-hop culture. Christians who had been raised in urban environments had no home. They didn't fit in at most churches, but they understood our music. Now they felt like they could love rap *and* love Jesus without compromising anything.

We posted the album on a music website, and people around the country now had a chance to hear what we were producing. The sound was so different from anything else being released at the time that the album started to penetrate the market. We received orders from across Texas; and before long, Ben and I were licking envelopes and mailing CDs to Oklahoma, Louisiana, Arkansas and then, all over the country.

The music was gaining momentum, the fan base was growing, and everything seemed to be soaring. But as the music flowed out, there was only one problem: I kept getting in the way.

131

★ ★ ★

My earliest music turned out a lot like my early efforts to evangelize. It was rooted in pure intentions and a true expression of what I believed, but my own self-righteousness and insecurities kept getting in the way.

During this period of my life, I was what the apostle Paul called "a Pharisee of Pharisees." I was leading Bible studies, volunteering with troubled youth, putting all the money I made from shows into a non-profit, and even moved into the inner city. When it came to following Jesus, I felt like I was doing it right. As a result, the music rarely portrayed me as someone who was broken or in need of spiritual growth. Instead, I was always the hero in the music. In these early songs, the example of what it looked like to live right was almost always me.

One of my biggest points of pride, for example, was how many mission trips I took. It was as if the number of stamps in my passport was a measure of how committed I was to Christ. So, I sang in "Go Hard":

> *Went to Asia had to duck and hide for sharin my faith*
> *They tell me water it down when I get back to States*
> *They say tone the music down you might sell a lot of*
> *records*
> *But it's people out here dying and none of 'em heard the*
> *message*

Going on mission trips is a noble thing, of course. But my motivation was off. I was proud of myself, and I wanted others to be proud of me too. The subtle message in the music was "You need to be like me."

My self-righteousness not only affected the way I portrayed myself in the music, it also influenced the way I sang about others. Because *I* was making sacrifices and *I* was on fire and *I* was sold out and *I* was committed, sometimes I didn't have much grace for anyone who wasn't living like me. Hip-hop has historically been raw and confrontational, but it was like I was getting in the faces of people who disagreed with me or weren't 100 percent committed to God.

- Whats up
- Who DAT
- It's me again the one you used to call ya friend. I know you aint forgot me?
- Yeah you always got me caught in sin
- Here you go hit that agin. You act like me aint cool or somethin lets go smoke a kool or somethin talk & sip a brew or sumthin
- Nah I aint trustin you it aint nothin but lust in you Thanks be to God I obeyed the teaching I was entrusted to/ Cause when you pass by you just want me to back slide have me feelin sick like I'm comin down off a crack high
- Man thats a flat lie you act like I'm the Bad guy Ya know when me & you got together we had a Corand time/ lets take it all the back t'd like the 6th Grade the last thing on Ya mind was tryna live Saved/ Remember house parties rember & kissing in the Dark That was Just inndent fun come on
- Dont Start/ See Dawg I live by the spirit so I don't Gratify all of your

sinful desires that never satisfy //
kill Dat look me in my face
and tell me I'mma lie
fa aint like chasing women Gettin
Drunk & Gettin High Gettin
Money Stayin fly
Liven up the playas life
he was havin fun now you tryna
be religious Guy /
First of all lower yo voice
who you talkin to?/ Hard cutted
August 02 I got caught wit your
TRUCK flip over on 35 thats was
all from you I'll mess around
& lose my life tryna walk in
you/ I'm standin on stages &
Got these people believin me /
What I look like trying Gratify
this disease in me/
So now I'm a disease man
please I Got ya back Dawg
~~Hse lil~~
I aint sayin ~~drop that~~ Jesus
& be rap star / All I'm sayin
is When it's you & me lets be real
folk

We aint gotta be sellin drugs
2 torne kill folks / mybe js
a lil...
- what?! A lil this a lil
that a lil BET late @ night
~~becomes~~ it's like a lil crack
but see you aint bare lie to me
- Oh I see how you're tryin ~~~~?
- Bet tonite becomes addiction to
pornography / And thats in no
way honoring the GOD whose
ruling soverignly /
- A~~~~ S~~~~ you miss old times
- yeah possibly but after that I
Sober up a think of Jesus holdin
up HIS skin on the Cross for
the Drunken nights I was throwin
Every thought of blowin up is
Captured in His flowin blood /
I start ~~thinkin~~ Philipians 4:8
when you showin up
- You know I aint sore quit...
- Yeah I know but I am Dead to
~~And~~ one day I'll ~~~~ present with
Jesus who died & bled for you.
Colossans 1:15 thats the God that
I trust in the father crushed

Him but in doing So He has
Crushed Sin

135

Few things, for example, wound me up more than "prosperity gospel" preachers and churches. In one song I even inserted a line that subtly attacked a prominent church by name. It was true, but it was still a pot shot, and it wasn't gracious. My words indicted an entire church community, many of whom sincerely love Jesus and are imperfectly trying to follow Him. I never considered that there were sincere and godly people who attended that church who might be affected by words, but years later I met one. "I am a big fan of yours," he said, "but that song really hurt me."

I almost never perform that song anymore, and if I do, I don't sing that line. Not because I don't still believe the truth of what I said—I do—but because I've learned to temper the truth with grace.

★ ★ ★

In addition to self-righteousness, my music was influenced by my own insecurities and need for acceptance. I wanted for people to tell me I was good enough and to feel like I was a part of a community. As the music became more popular, the fan base expanded from urban communities into conservative, white suburban Christian communities. Suddenly, I was being invited to perform at megachurches and being recognized by prominent pastors.

It felt good to have strong, male Christian figures I respected throw their arms around me and pat me on my back, and this started to influence the music. As I read books by these pastors, and other great Christian thinkers from the past, the lofty truths I was encountering began to show up in my lyrics. This fueled their acceptance of me because there weren't many rappers condensing the theology of Charles Spurgeon or A. W. Tozer and inserting it into a four-minute track.

When I released the song "Souled Out," for example, I rapped the following lines:

> *We were slaves to sinful ways but Christ freed us, believe*
> *us*
> *Because of the bible that supersedes us*
> *Not to the intellectual thesis*
> *They say we believe in a fool's faith 'cause kids can grasp*
> *it*
> *And salvation is granted, to those who ask it*
> *But even if you don't know systematic theology or*
> *eschatology*
> *You know Jesus is who you ought to seek*

137

After singing this at a show, a fan who was in divinity school asked me where I was enrolled in seminary. I wasn't, of course, but the fact that he even assumed I might be made me feel respected. Deep down, I was checking certain theological boxes in songs now and then to keep winning the approval of others.

While my motivation was off, it wasn't totally off. Part of me was just doing what I'd seen done by similar musicians. There were only a few role models at the time for a rapper who was also a Christian. I looked to William Branch, aka "The Ambassador," who was the lead for the hip-hop group Cross Movement. We called him "Deuce," and he was a pastoral theologian by nature. He was even attending Dallas Theological Seminary at the time. When he rapped, his lyrics had a certain theological depth. That was just who he naturally was.

Few people could use the language of urban culture while also speaking pastoral truths in music. But Deuce saw himself as a missionary to hip-hop culture. He became something of a pastor to me and other people who connected with his music. His messages had authority in our eyes.

138

London Aug 08

It's been a blessing being on tour I have seen God work in amazing ways & wondered how & why He uses such lowly unworthy vessels. My sin of course is the source of my heart break but lately the routine of concerts & ministry brought me to the sin of trusting in myself, not to mention the sin of pride. It's shown its face in strange & inconspicuous ways in the past but now it's so blatant. Such obvious envy such disturbing arrogance that I'm sickened by it. At times I want humility but not at the cost of prestige & popularity. I know I need more of God but I feel I've found myself ~~~~~~~~ feeling my identity is wrapped up in people loving me. Take that away Lord I don't care if I no longer the Next best thing as long as I'm content w/ You in process. Show me yourself God. More of You. I need to Get more of You. Grow me Move me into a place of incredible growth water me Lord & increase my desire to know You & serve You. Conform me more to Your image. In Jesus name May I die daily & live anew in You.

Amen.

The problem was that I was not Deuce. I had different gifts and different talents and different passions and a different calling. For one thing, I was more of a "lamenter" than a "pastor" by nature. While Deuce's music felt like the epistles of Paul, my natural gifts would have yielded something more like the psalms. But there was no category for that at the time among rappers who were Christian. So instead of allowing myself to produce music naturally, according to the way God designed me, I was fighting to fit another mold.

Operating as a "Pastor Rapper" was hard work for me because it wasn't playing to my strengths. Rather than letting the music pour out of me when the inspiration came, I would spend hours studying beforehand. I would read books and commentaries like I was preparing to give a sermon and *then* I would rap. I felt like if I wasn't teaching, preaching, reciting Scripture, and evangelizing through my music, I wasn't doing it right. Being theologically educated is a great thing. And using music to explicitly express theology is needed. But I mistakenly believed it was the only way to make music.

On rare occasion, however, I would let go and let the "lamenter" in me come out. When I did—when I let Lecrae just be Lecrae—it would spark magic. I wrote a song called "Praying For You" in which I let go of my insecurities and self-righteousness for a minute and just allowed myself to express what I felt. Unlike some of my other songs, I wasn't preaching at people or telling them what to do or stop doing. I just told the story of a broken person who had fallen on hard times:

139

> *Father, I'm prayin' for a friend he and I are pretty close,*
> *and out of all my friends for this one I'm concerned the*
> *most.*
> *He say he readin' daily but he ain't really learnin'.*
> *He been in church but say that he ain't moved by any*
> *sermon.*

The lyrics are raw as I rap about the struggles of this man. He feels the pull of materialism and greed. He's not always a loving husband to his wife. He wrestles with worry and anxiety about the future. His spiritual life isn't what it should be, and he has a hard time trusting God. And then comes the song's surprise ending:

> *God I know it's killin' You because it's killin' me*
> *and matter of fact there's somethin' else he's concealin'*
> *see, the person that I've been prayin' about is really me . . .*

Rather than make myself the winner, I allowed myself to be the loser. Rather than set myself up as a hero, I admitted that I'm often the villain. Rather than hide my struggles, I shared my struggles. Rather than force myself to preach, I allowed myself to express what I was feeling. The feedback I got from fans was incredible. People wrote to say how much that song impacted them because it was real and vulnerable. And this was one of the first moments I began to wonder if maybe God was

WHEN PEOPLE ASK ME IF I REGRET THE MUSIC I PRODUCED EARLY IN MY CAREER, I DON'T HESITATE. NO, ABSOLUTELY NOT.

calling me to make a shift in my music and begin producing new songs that were truer to how I was naturally made.

When people ask me if I regret the music I produced early in my career, I don't hesitate. No, absolutely not. Everything I said in those songs was true. I never lied or used the music to manipulate people. The songs on all of those albums were snapshots of my heart during those moments in my life. But even though it was all true, it was often rooted in the wrong motivations or disconnected from my natural giftedness.

Luckily, we serve a God who can use our imperfect efforts to serve Him—despite our insecurities, despite our self-righteousness, despite our shortsightedness. As a friend of mine said to me, "God can draw a straight line with a crooked stick."[12] And He did. God was using the music to transform lives, to break down walls, and to impact communities.

As the music gained momentum, I started to think God was preparing to change me. But before God could change me, He needed to mature me. And before God could mature me, He needed to move me.

9 - MEMPHIS MOMENT

I took my girl from the lone star to Memphis, Tenn
on them cold blocks
And what you think we moved for, to see kids
get killed in the school zone
To see crack get sold, bodies turned cold
What do you think, I think that's cool, bro?
And why do you think I went to school for?
To turn around and move back to the hood?
Nah, boy, that's what it's called a sacrifice,
this is bigger than me, it's for a greater good.

Lecrae | "Sacrifice" | *Church Clothes*

After my first album took off, the music started making money. People were asking me to come to their churches, or conferences—or whatever event—and after performing, they would give me a hundred bucks or so for my time.

This began happening more frequently, and I started thinking about quitting my job at the cable company to focus on the music. I crunched the numbers and determined I could survive on about $500 per month to cover rent, food, and some gas. At twenty-five years old, I took the leap and stepped into my dream of being a full-time hip-hop artist.

My universe seemed to be coming together. I had regular income to pay my bills. My spiritual life was steady and strong. I was finding purpose through leading a Bible study, volunteering at the detention center, and building community with James and my other Christian friends. And the music was connecting with more people each day.

But something was still missing.

I felt a stirring in my spirit. A restlessness. An aloneness. I wanted more. I needed more. I was made for more.

It has been true since the beginning of time: "It is not good for man to be alone." I was sick of being single, and the desire for marriage was growing stronger.

My frustration led me to confess what I felt to Calvin, a pastor friend of mine. I told him that my experience with women in the past made me nervous about my ability to find a good woman. What should I do? Calvin told me that I was looking for the wrong thing. Ultimately, I didn't need a *good* woman; I needed a *godly* woman. This meant finding someone who loved Jesus, had a servant's heart, and respected the godly men in her life. Calvin encouraged me not to engage a woman's heart until I found a woman like this and was ready to commit to her.

He was right about needing to find a godly woman, but the attributes he listed were a tall order. Even if I could find her, how would I convince her to marry someone with a past like mine? Who would want someone with my history? With my issues? With my flaws? With my instability? Finding a godly girl would take an act of God.

I prayed for God to bring a woman like Calvin described into my life. I got real with God and told Him exactly what I was feeling and asked Him to lead the kind of woman I needed to me. I asked God for each attribute, starting with a love for Christ. But in the midst of asking, I had a revolutionary thought: what if the girl I was praying for was already here? While I desperately wanted God to do something *for* me, maybe I needed to trust in what God was already doing *around* me.

I thought about the women I knew who were godly, and one named Darragh came to mind. She was attractive, energetic, fun to be around, and beautiful inside and out. She was adventurous and always willing to do new things. And she was also godly. I had met her through a campus Bible study, and she loved Jesus as much as any woman I knew. Darragh had a servant's heart, and we had volunteered at several ministries together over the years. She also had a respect for godly men. Her father was a quintessential, almost perfect dad, a minister in his church and a respected fireman who is also warm and caring. Growing up in her house had taught her to recognize and respect godly men.

But just as important, I had no doubt that Darragh could handle my past. I'd known her for nearly seven years, a period during which I had struggled with waves of . . .

Pride.

Depression.

Anxiety.

Insecurity.

Drugs.

Sex.

Indifference.

Restlessness.

Anger.

Legalism.

Self-righteousness.

Self-worthlessness.

Selfishness.

Ambition.

Darragh had seen me at my high points and low points, on my best days and worst. I had cycled between faith and doubt, clarity and confusion, hope in God and complete despair. She chose to stay my friend through it all. One of Darragh's greatest strengths is faithfulness, which explains why she had remained during my roller coaster ride. My craziness couldn't destroy her faithfulness.

I thought about it. And prayed about it. Then thought some more. And then prayed some more. Finally, I picked up the phone and nervously dialed her number.

"Darragh . . . uh . . . so, I've known you for seven years. And, we're like, good friends and whatever. But, um, I think you're the type of person I'd like to spend the rest of my life with," I said. "So . . . I was thinking . . . I was thinking I would like to pursue you with the intention of marriage."

I could hear her smiling through the phone.

Four months later, I proposed. And four months after that, we were married.

Looking back, it amazes me how many important moments Darragh had been a part of. She was in the campus Bible study when I first wandered in. She was at the Praise Parties I had attended out of sheer boredom.

She was with me on the bus ride to Atlanta, singing with everyone else. She sat in the same service where I fell to my knees and asked God to forgive me. She had seen me return to campus on fire and then watched as the flame of faith almost flickered out.

I wasn't initially interested in her because, as a confused eighteen-year-old, I thought she was "too Christian" for me. But God had kept us close to each other as He prepared our hearts and grew our character.

When I asked Darragh to marry me, I remember giving her a full disclaimer so there was no doubt about what she was getting into. I reminded her of my past—all of which she knew—and I told her that I wasn't going to be a predictable husband.

"If you marry someone like me, it means you might have to go through hell because I am willing to push limits and boundaries to be whatever God wants me to be," I said. "If God calls me to be homeless and live under a bridge or to move to a faraway place, I'm going to do that."

Darragh affirmed the thought. She said that's what she loved about me and she trusted me no matter what God called us to. I told her that I loved her too and would always protect her. But words are cheap, and our commitment to them was about to be tested.

★ ★ ★

His name was Soup Campbell. Well, it was actually Roy, but that's what everyone called him. Soup was six-foot-three-inches tall and a former pro baseball player. I first met Soup at a Bible study in Texas where he had come as a guest speaker to talk about the program he was leading in

Memphis. He and several others lived in one of the worst inner-city neighborhoods in Tennessee, where they were mentoring kids to be leaders and living out their faith in radical ways.

"Let me tell you something: we don't do that sissy Christian stuff. We don't put on no white gloves and collect gum at the front door of the church," Soup said. "We do real Christian man stuff. If you want to be in the hood where you might get shot for what you believe or jump out of planes in countries where being a Christian is illegal, then come join my team."

His tough talk was exactly the kind of thing that naturally drew someone like me who had never had a male role model. Plus, I'd been feeling for some time that I needed to move to a place where I could really grow and test my faith. I started to think maybe I needed to move to Memphis and join Soup Campbell.

I matured as a Christian by listening to sermons that others had recommended. I sat in on seminary classes on occasion, and I read books by great thinkers and pastors like John Piper, John Wesley, C. S. Lewis, Martin Luther King Jr., and Fredrick Douglass. My passion to impact the world was becoming an unquenchable fire. I hadn't been further east than Tennessee, let alone outside of America, and I wanted to reach the world with the truth that had set me free.

When I told Darragh that I thought we might need to move to Memphis, she was surprisingly open. She hadn't been raised in the hood, but she was serving in an inner-city ministry mentoring girls at the time. So she had an idea of what it would be like.

How would this affect my music career? I didn't really care. I just wanted to grow in my faith and be used by God.

Playing some video games during my college years. Now is probably a good time to apologize to everyone who witnessed my wardrobe during this period of life.

Hanging with my Aunt Cathy. During this phase, I was always wearing a size 5-XL in everything.

Hanging with my in-laws in Dallas the night I proposed to my wife, Darragh. She was shocked. Her Dad, Buford, was proud . . . and I was honored.

This is my wife and me on a mission trip to Honduras in 2006. We fought every night and preached Jesus every day.

Never too busy with my career to overlook the Great Commission. I'm in Beijing, China, here. Everyone on the streets thought I was Kobe Bryant.

Napping with my first son, David. The tatt on my arm is Tupac-inspired and bad. But this moment was good.

I've got a box of CD's under my arm, which I carried store to store. I was hustlin' legally!

Rapping at a concert in Houston 2006. In case you're wondering, I'm wearing my cousin's "clothing line."

"I am Tim Tebow in the fourth quarter, they can't hold me." Lyrics I wrote for Trip Lee's song "I'm Good."

At the Billboard Awards with Akon. I asked him if I could borrow $20 million, and he said he'd get back to me. Still waiting man . . .

Everyone needs a shepherd for your soul. I have been blessed with many pastors in my life.

Bubba Watson and Jordin Sparks are two good friends I'm still honored to know and regularly see to this day.

Me and my mom.

Visiting my old house in Memphis in 2015. It was a
tough neighborhood, but I had many good memories
there. Never forget your roots.

Grammy Award Ceremony

Mi familia. They are the priority.

* * *

Darragh and I both felt like it would be good for us to move away from our families at the outset of our marriage to be on our own and establish our lives independently from anyone else. The only question was how two poor newlyweds could find the money to up and move their entire lives 488 miles across the country.

But when God is taking you somewhere, He usually opens the door. You only have to be willing to walk when He does. The door opened for us when Ben's friend in Memphis helped us get a grant from a private donor to pay for our move into the community. Before I knew it, I, Darragh, and all of our belongings were on our way. Not long after we settled into our tiny cul-de-sac house on Mimosa Avenue in the Binghampton neighborhood, Darragh and I realized just how much we would need God's help.

On the one hand, Memphis was a time of blessing for us both. My wife started teaching reading classes at the local community center. A child's options are severely limited by a poor education, and Darragh was determined to help the children in our neighborhood keep their options open by learning to read on their grade level. She mentored girls in the neighborhood, teaching them basic life skills and being the big sister many needed but didn't have.

I started coaching a basketball team and connecting with the kids in the neighborhood. When I looked into many of the kids' eyes, I would see myself. Many lived in fatherless homes, raised by an overwhelmed mother who was doing all she could to provide a better life for her kids than she had. Most of them were really wrestling with their identities, trying to act hard to cover up the confusion and insecurities they felt. By stepping into their lives, I felt like I was stepping back in time and stepping into my own life.

I was determined to be for these kids what I needed but never had: a strong male figure who they could look up to, confide in, and lean on. But my ultimate goal wasn't to be their friend. I wanted to help shape their character and raise them to be leaders.

I wanted to help these boys become men by giving them a different vision of what the future could look like and challenging them to choose a better path. Once some boys from the neighborhood stopped by my house after school and asked about the strange pictures of me and Darragh where she was wearing a white dress and I was in a tux. They had never seen a wedding before. So I showed them a video of my wedding ceremony and talked to them about what committing to a spouse forever looked like.

Darragh and I were always serving people. We mowed neighbors' lawns, fixed old ladies' houses, and worked to build relationships with everyone in between. From innocent grade-school children to roughneck drug dealers, this work looked nothing like the in-your-face evangelism I was doing back in Texas. It was harder, slower, and much more complicated. But I was seeing God transform more hearts and lives than ever before. Our community was changing, and my wife and I felt fulfilled and humbled to be a part of it. We loved our friends there, and the quality of Binghampton was improving because of the resilience of its residents.

But living in Memphis wasn't a dream. In some ways, our first year there was a nightmare. The level of crime in our neighborhood was more intense than anything Darragh or I had faced before. We slept on the floor at night because gunfire was ringing outside and we didn't want to get hit by a stray bullet while sleeping in bed.

Several of our friends died while we were in Memphis. My neighbor was stabbed to death by thieves. Another friend, who was battling a drug addiction, stole some money and got shot. A thirty-three-year-old man in the neighborhood committed a mass murder in the streets, killing half a dozen people, including small children. One of the kids I was coaching went to prison for shooting someone in the face.

The hardest tragedy we experienced was when my close friend D. Wade died. He grew up in the North Memphis projects and had taken a bullet or two there. D. Wade helped me navigate the Memphis streets and culture. He was a basketball buddy of mine who came to know Jesus and had just gotten married. He was really changing his life around and becoming a mentor in the community. And then D. Wade died. I didn't know exactly how to process a close friend dying like that.

To combat the pressures of the inner city, I became consumed with serving. I increasingly traveled and performed at churches and Christian conferences. I once performed twenty-seven shows in a single month. It was a lot of work, but people's lives were being transformed. I was flying around the world taking mission trips—Asia, Africa, Central America—and I was seeing God change lives there too. And when I was in town, I was coaching or mentoring or studying. This was all good, of course, but it meant that I was failing to pour into my marriage.

Darragh is a quality time person, but I'm not. I've always been something of a lone wolf. So when I was traveling, I didn't bother to call and check in or even give consideration to what she might need while I was away. And when I was home, I wasn't making up for it. I felt like if we had a good day or so together each week, that was enough.

Worse, when we were together, my self-righteousness often spoiled our time together. I was so consumed with looking good that I would criticize her for talking too much or challenging me in public in any way. Because I saw her as a reflection of myself, I was trying to manage her instead of loving her enough to let her be who God made her to be. My behavior made Darragh hesitant to open up and to fully invest in our marriage. I wasn't cultivating trust or creating consistency. I wasn't loving her well. I was trying to be a good person in the world, but I was failing to be a godly husband to my wife.

This led to fights. Big fights. Shouting and screaming and slamming doors. She would blame me, and I would blame her. And I'd always end up confused.

"I moved to Memphis to serve you, God," I prayed. "We've made more sacrifices than I can count for you. So why is life so hard?"

Eventually, I realized that I would lose my wife's heart if I didn't change. We got help from godly friends and a good counselor who helped us repair our marriage. But it was a long process and exhausting work, especially with everything else happening around us.

153

So there I was—a newlywed husband struggling to make my marriage work, a fired-up Christian trying to serve Jesus in one of the most murderous cities in America, and a musician struggling to understand who I am as an artist. My life was chaotic and purposeful, amazing and awful, all at once. As it turns out, this was a perfect environment for God to break me down and build me up. And that's exactly what God did.

★ ★ ★

Being in Christian "boot camp" in Memphis was not just an act of service. It was also a process of learning. I attended a Bible institute there with some of my friends to learn theology, philosophy, and church history. But I was also learning about culture and the Christian calling to understand, engage, and transform it.

Like many believers, I'd never considered what it meant to influence culture in an authentically Christian way. Sure, in Texas, I'd gotten in people's grills to tell them they needed to repent. And yes, in Memphis, I'd worked to serve an inner-city community. And, of course, I'd been on more mission trips than most people I knew. But I'd never thought much about what it meant to be a cultural change agent, to be "salt" and "light" in the world. My deficiency was immediately apparent to one of my teachers at the Bible institute.

"You don't have a biblical worldview," he told me.

I was shocked and speechless.

What are you talking about, man? Look at all the stamps in my passport. Do you know how many mission trips I've been on? Look at my resume. I've written dozens of songs that talk about Jesus. Look at everything I'm doing in this neighborhood. I am serving kids that most people have forgotten about. How can you say I don't have a biblical worldview?

Once my head stopped spinning and I cooled off, I was left with a humbling thought: I couldn't actually define the term "biblical worldview." I had read the Bible and memorized my share of verses. I knew what Christianity said about conversion but not what it taught about culture. Like a lot of Christians, my knowledge of Scripture was mostly limited to what it said about getting "saved" and following the "rules." But also like a lot of Christians, I hadn't spent much time considering what it meant to see the world through God's eyes.

Like a ship commissioned for its maiden voyage, I launched out in a relentless pursuit to understand what the heck a "biblical worldview" looked like. I started devouring books on the topic, and three shook me especially hard.

The first was Nancy Pearcey's book *Total Truth: Liberating Christianity from Its Cultural Captivity*. Pearcey is something of an expert on what it means to have a biblical worldview. She studied under Francis Schaeffer and co-authored several books with Charles Colson (both men talked a lot about the importance of having a Christian worldview).

Total Truth challenged the notion that following Jesus is a purely private spiritual matter. It attacked the false division between the "sacred" and the "secular," as well as the "private" and the "public." Christian principles are meant to saturate our lives, she says, and flow out into the world around us.

"Having a Christian worldview means being utterly convinced that biblical principles are not only true but also work better in the grit and grime of the real world," Pearcey wrote.[13]

Rather than only speaking to salvation and sanctification, Pearcey taught me that being a Christian empowers us to influence the broader culture. Rather than just teaching us how to get saved, live holy lives, and evangelize non-Christians, a biblical worldview shapes how we think

> **FOLLOWING JESUS DOESN'T JUST SAVE US *FROM* A LESS FULFILLING LIFE OR ETERNAL SEPARATION FROM GOD. IT ALSO SAVES US *TO* A LIFE THAT CAN RADICALLY TRANSFORM THE WORLD AROUND US THROUGH THE POWER OF GOD.**

155

about politics, business, law, education, and the arts. The Christian faith is not just a religious truth, she said, but the total truth about all reality.

Pearcey taught me that being a Christian is not just about being saved *from* something but also being saved *to* something. Following Jesus doesn't just save us *from* a less fulfilling life or eternal separation from God. It also saves us *to* a life that can radically transform the world around us through the power of God.

My mind aint a slippin / I'm slippin back
into Darkness / means I now Dwell
with Killas Dealas and heartless /
Yeah That ex-Con was chillin in
FRONT YARD / Talkin bout how made
30 large from sellia hard / walk down
the Block with a dude sippin then
he step off bought himself a
twenty then then / Instead
Yellin on him
like "PAGAN. You Live in 'Sin'"
I told em hit me up we'll
go hoopin around (off
Instead of Complainin how the whole
world is filthy / we need to come
to Grips that we all were guilty /
but God has sealed me / HIS stripes
have healed me of the Sin sickness /
that controlled and killed me /
I don't smoke, hard / or
Chese nore ller with Curves /
or Sip thunder bird until my words
are slurred / I do like rap were
hats & have caps / And I like
my clothes big and hangin off IC
my back.

Where Nancy Pearcey left off, Andy Crouch picked up. While Pearcey convinced me that Christians were responsible for transforming culture, Crouch equipped me with a way to do it.

In *Culture Making: Recovering Our Creative Calling*, Crouch says that most Christians relate to culture in four ways. Most of the time, we just *consume* culture without thinking much about what we're taking in. We can also *critique* or outright *condemn* culture when it operates according to values that don't line up with our own. Or when we find culture alluring, but are uncomfortable with really engaging with it, we can *copy* culture. This is the approach that produces Christian films and Christian schools and Christian T-shirts and any other "Christian" version of something—yes, that includes Christian music. None of these approaches are sufficient, Crouch says. The only way to truly transform culture is to *create* culture.[14]

Pearcey's book led me to Crouch's book, and now Crouch's book led me to the "Good Book." And this was when everything changed for me.

★ ★ ★

Rereading the Gospels, I was struck by how Jesus was constantly interacting with culture and the people who existed outside of religious structures. Tax collectors, prostitutes, Gentiles—these were his favorite dinner companions. When I got to the Sermon on the Mount, I noticed that Jesus commanded His followers to be "salt" and "light." How can Christians be salt and light if they never encounter meat and darkness? They can't.

But the biggest revelation for me occurred when I was on tour working through a DVD teaching series and studying the sixteenth chapter of Matthew's Gospel. In a town called Caesarea Philippi, Jesus asks Simon Peter who the disciple believes He is. A prophet? A miracle worker? An influential teacher?

"You are the Messiah, the Son of the Living God,"[15] the disciple says.

And then Jesus offers Peter a strange reply: "Blessed are you, Simon son of Jonah! For flesh and blood have not revealed this to you, but my father in heaven. And I tell you, you are Peter, and on this rock, I will build my church, and the gates of Hell will not prevail against it."[16]

I used to believe this meant that nothing would destroy the church, not even the most evil forces in the world. It was as if God wrapped His big arms around the church like a fortress and was keeping all the bad people and bad things away from it. But when I studied the passage this time, I saw it differently.

GOD DOES NOT WANT TO BUILD BARRIERS AROUND THE CHURCH; HE WANTS TO BUILD BRIDGES TO THE CULTURE SO THE GOSPEL CAN FLOOD INTO IT.

Caesarea Philippi was a hedonistic place in the ancient world. It was a place that wasn't friendly to God-followers, a place where "hell" reigned supreme. So Jesus is standing there in the midst of a godless city and pointing to the culture around Him and saying, "Upon *this* rock, in the middle of this sinful place where people do not worship God, I'm going to work. Right in the midst of all this mess!"

Interestingly, Jesus doesn't just mention hell, but the *gates* of hell. Gates are not weapons; they don't attack people or things. They are defenses. They are designed to keep people or things out. I used to believe that Jesus was promising to keep hell out of the church, but He was actually teaching that hell was powerless to keep His church out of it. God does not want to build barriers around the church; He wants to build bridges to the culture so the Gospel can flood into it.

Sitting on that tour bus, I had my own Caesarea Philippi moment. I could no longer assume that Christianity only affected the way I saw salvation or sanctification; I needed to accept that it was the total truth about the world. I could no longer condemn, critique, copy, or mindlessly consume culture; I needed to begin creating culture as a child of the Great Creator. And I could no longer sit comfortably inside my Christian subculture and thank God that He was keeping hell away. It was time to leave the religious ghetto and kick down hell's front door.

10 -
KICKING
DOWN
HELL'S
DOOR

I'm what happens when Outkast meets the writings of Moses
The views are opposing, but they correlate
And me and Christ don't match, but we coordinate
If Wu-Tang can spit five percent gems
I can talk about Him who died for my sins
I'm not a gospel rapper, not a holy roller
I'm just a product of grace, spreading hope to the hopeless

Lecrae | "Co-Sign" | *Church Clothes*

Art is nothing if not a reflection of the artist. My worldview had transformed. It was only a matter of time before the music followed.

I was mostly making music for Christians in the early days. Over time, some sub-groups developed. There were Christian kids from urban contexts. And there were conservative evangelical Christians from the suburbs.

And there were "Reformed" Christians who liked me because their favorite theologian or pastor gave me his stamp of approval. But in the end, the fans were almost all Christians.

Nothing is inherently wrong with making art for a specific audience, and in my case, it worked out pretty well. I allowed my prophetic side to come out, telling the truth about matters when some others were afraid to speak up. Even though my self-righteousness was getting in the way, people could smell the authenticity and passion. Lives were being changed.

But the more I discerned my calling, the more convinced I was that God didn't want me to just make music for the church. Christian culture was never in my DNA anyway. I wasn't raised in it. I didn't know it. I never felt fully comfortable in it. I wasn't some church kid who was trying to be hip-hop because it was cool; I was a kid who grew up in hip-hop who was making music as a Christian.

I had a heart for reaching people who were far from God. Even my misguided attempts at evangelism hinted at that. But the music was never coming into contact with those people. Outside of the church, I didn't exist. I was invisible.

It occurred to me that even if people outside the church were to stumble upon my music, they'd probably dismiss it. They wouldn't understand the theological language that I was inserting to please Christian leaders. They would have smelled the self-righteousness and how I was always the song's hero. The "be better," "do better," "work harder" messages in the music would never transform them. The Gospel naturally offends those outside of the faith. But I wanted people to be loved, not guilted, into following Jesus.

In addition to sensing a call to reach people inside *and* outside the church, everything I was learning was pushing me to influence the broader society. I remember reading a story about how Christians built some of the first professional hospitals. They saw a need, and they addressed it. By creating something new, they were on the cutting edge of transforming the way humans thought about healthcare. How could this way of thinking change the way I was creating my art?

For years I'd lived in communities drowning in social problems and sin: fatherlessness, sexism, racism, poverty, violence. These communities were filled with people who didn't know how to deal with their emotions, didn't understand systemic oppression, and weren't being educated on basic economics and personal finance. I loved going on mission trips. I loved mentoring kids and repairing old ladies' houses. I loved meeting needs in the hood. But my music—one of the greatest assets for impacting culture—never came into contact with the world outside of the church. It was like I was cleaning up the oil spill when I should have been climbing onto the tanker and plugging the hole. The music gave me an opportunity to get upstream of culture and produce art with messages that could shape the broader society.

Yet most of the music was doing nothing to improve the problems I was witnessing. At its best, my music was trying to push Christians to live right. By God's grace, some people were coming to faith through the music. But there was nothing in it to inspire them to apply their faith to the world's complex problems. I had been focused

163

on behavior modification, not worldview transformation. So there I was, a musician in the midst of troubled urban culture failing to properly use the gifts God gave me to address the problems around me.

As I prayed about what God wanted for the next season of my life, I began to feel that God was not just wanting to change me as a person, but He also wanted to move me to a new place.

I considered Philadelphia and Los Angeles and New York City, but something kept drawing me toward Atlanta. Hip-hop coming out of different cities has its own distinct sound, often unrecognizable to the untrained ear. My music had always had a Southern feel, so Atlanta seemed like a good fit. Additionally, I wanted to go to a place where culture was being shaped. When it came to hip-hop, few cities were more influential than Atlanta.

I HAD BEEN FOCUSED ON BEHAVIOR MODIFICATION, NOT WORLDVIEW TRANSFORMATION.

164

The problem with a lot of popular hip-hop is that it often glorifies the worst aspects of humanity. It can celebrate violence, even murder. It sometimes promotes misogynistic attitudes and the objectification of women. It can devalue education, glorify sex, and idolize wealth. It's difficult to completely blame these artists—many are just singing what they know and creating what people are consuming. But I began to dream about what it might mean if a different brand of hip-hop artists were to exist in the same space while creating music with alternative values. In a matter of months, Darragh and I were packing our belongings into cardboard boxes and preparing to relocate.

Moving to a new place wouldn't automatically transform the music. I needed to unchain my creative side—
not just to evangelize, but to paint an alternative picture
of the world that was both saturated by the gospel and
accessible enough for anyone.

As I dreamed, fear crept in. The voices in my head
began to taunt me. To tell me not to follow my calling.
They said that my Christian fans wouldn't understand, that
they would abandon me. When this didn't stick, the voices
began to speak to my insecurities and lifelong struggle for
acceptance. They told me that non-Christian audiences
would never accept me. Not as an artist. I wasn't good
enough to make music for the masses, the voices said. Even
if I was, the music would never influence culture.

I was confident enough in God's calling to beat back
the voices of doubt and despair. But when the voices disappeared, all I heard was silence. I had spent years producing another kind of art. I could do it in my sleep. But now
I didn't know what to write. I'd sit and stare at blank pages.
I wanted to be vulnerable, but the thought of expressing
myself this way left me paralyzed.

For months I felt stuck in a dark place with my hands
tied. But one day I decided to sit down and just write.
Whatever came to mind. Whatever I was feeling. Whatever
I was wrestling with. I couldn't see the way forward, but I
decided to start walking anyway. And out of the darkness,
a new kind of album was birthed.

★ ★ ★

The house was empty the day I started to write again.
My family was running errands, so it was more quiet than

normal. There was barely any furniture, except a wooden kitchen table where I sat and stared at a blank page. I had learned so much about how to be an effective Christian that I had forgotten how to be an effective songwriter. Creating the music requires more than hard work and perseverance. It needs a spark, a flash, a flame to kindle the creative process.

Just write, Lecrae.

I had just released what many of my fans felt was one of my best albums, *Rebel*. It was full of strong, bold, and challenging content. Its quality was on par with current hip-hop, due to the contributions of some of the most talented producers I know, Joseph Prielozny and Gabriel "GAWVI" Azucena.

Just start writing.

To write *Rebel*, I had gone back to San Diego to write most of the album so I could feel connected with my roots and the common struggles of humanity. The album struck a chord with most of the listeners, and many have said it's one of the albums that helped shape their lives. Still, there were only a couple of transparent and relatable songs that connected to a world outside of Christian circles.

Write whatever comes to mind.

I had been stuck for so long, I just started writing about what being stuck felt like. The frustration, the silence, the darkness. As my hands moved, words started coming to me. But slowly. It was like greasing the gears of a machine that's been sitting idle. If you listen to one of the first songs I wrote, "Wish It Wasn't True," you can feel me struggling to get the words out:

> *Uhh, you I, umm,*
> *I know I just got out of rehab, but uh,*
> *I actually need to be checked back in. Yeah.*
> *I didn't think this was gonna happen to me . . . man . . .*
> *Feel like I'm back in that dark place*
> *Somewhere in between a rock and a hard place*
> *And I ain't doin nothin' bad, I'm just doin' bad*
> *Feelin' empty when I got more than I done ever had*
> *So Imma do what I do best when I feel depressed*
> *Go ahead and let my pen bleed out the stress*

Bleeding was a more accurate metaphor than I even realized at the time. God was pushing me to be real and let the true Lecrae spill into the lyrics. No more walls. No more holding back. No more guarding myself. No more casting myself as the hero. No more acting like I had it all together.

As I let go of pride and pretenses, the momentum increased. Soon, a different and deeper kind of music poured out of me. The breakout song on the album, "Background," admitted that I am sometimes tempted by the spotlight. I said that I don't deserve fame and glory— only God does. One song, "Killa," even confessed my battle with lust:

> *Walking to my grave letting evilness enslave me*
> *Evil looks so lovely covered in her lace of lies*
> *And the silky smooth seduction just manipulates my*
> *   mind*
> *Her fabric of fabrication is fueling my fascination*
> *While I'm intoxicated she starts her assassination*
> *I'm losing all my honor and my years to the merciless*
> *Giving all my life away but I'm just so immersed in this*

167

Writing the album felt like being back in that empty hospital room, seeking God for direction and scribbling with a crayon. I titled the album *Rehab*—not just because it reminded me of that vulnerable period in my life, but also because it expressed my deep need for personal, spiritual, and musical rehabilitation.

Rehab confessed my own self-righteousness and declared that I was unashamed of Jesus, yes. But I am also unashamed to admit my weaknesses. Unashamed to admit my brokenness. Unashamed to admit that I fail constantly and need help.

Most of the fans stuck with me through *Rehab*. Looking back, the album still had the residue of the Christian subculture on it and was littered with Christian-ese. It fit solidly in the Contemporary Christian Music genre. And it had a sort of pop sensibility that made it accessible. But even though it didn't totally line up with my new worldview, it was still a huge step forward in terms of authenticity. I was finally comfortable with being weak and imperfect in the music. I think of it almost as an artistic bridge between who I was and who I am.

The problem with bridges is that they get walked on from both sides. Secular critics didn't understand it because it felt so Christian. And many of my core Christian fans didn't understand it because it wasn't preachy. They were used to me playing the Pastor Rapper role. "Killa" never directly mentioned God or Jesus, and neither did "Background." So I lost some fans after the album released.

169

But I was confident I was moving in the direction God was calling. And I was also sure that this was only the beginning.

★ ★ ★

The authenticity of *Rehab* caught the attention of some mainstream influencers. And in 2011, I was invited to participate in the BET cypher. This is an event in conjunction with the BET Hip Hop Awards where some of the best young artists gather to rap sixteen bars and show off their talent. Those familiar with hip-hop know that this can make or break an artist.

The cypher took place in a warehouse in Brooklyn, and I didn't have much time to prepare. On the flight up and the hours preceding it, I was sweating. What would I say to a mainstream audience who wasn't familiar with me or my music? This was a watershed moment, so I knew I couldn't just spit a few lyrical bars like everyone else. Sure, I wanted to have a good delivery. But I also wanted to show people that you can be good at your craft and true to your faith at the same time. I wanted to show them that I was different, but I didn't want to shove Jesus down their throats. I eventually decided to just rap what I felt:

> *You probably watching like, man, I never heard of him*
> *I'll murder him*
> *The nerve of him*
> *Rocking with Premier, that's so absurd of him*
> *Wait until he spit a couple verbs at them*
> *If you really want to hate, wait,*
> *He got the Word with him*
> *I heard 'em holla "Jesus the Notorious,"*
> *No, The most glorious homie*

Some Christians who saw it weren't happy with me for using a Notorious B.I.G. reference to talk about Jesus and for giving a nod to DJ Premier, who has produced for most of mainstream hip-hop's elite artists. But I had just taken the same approach the Apostle Paul did in Acts 17. Our situations weren't that different. Paul had been invited to speak in the Areopagus, a place where all of the influential voices in his day gathered to trade ideas. In explaining what he believed, Paul used the language of culture and referenced their popular poets. I used the language of hip-hop, which I had spoken fluently since I was a kid, and I referenced some of our most prominent poet-rappers. When I flew home afterward, I felt at peace with my performance.

We had moved to Atlanta, and I started forming friendships with lots of non-Christian people. I struggled at first. I hadn't engaged with many non-Christians since coming to faith, except to argue with them about how sinful they were. Figuring out how to be friends with people who didn't believe in Jesus without compromising my beliefs was a process. I slowly learned how to love non-Christians without pushing them away. These relationships opened me up artistically, and I began to feel it was time to take another step forward.

I received a random phone call one day from a college friend named Street Symphony. We had lost touch, but he had gone on to become a producer and worked with mainstream artists from Ludacris to Rick Ross. Street told me that he had been swept up into the entertainment industry and the world of expensive cars, sex, and drugs. He felt empty. At some point, Street came across my music and he thought I might be able to help him think through life. He started wrestling with big questions about God and meaning. I would tell him what I believed and then let him work through what he believed. Over time, he saw that I wasn't full of judgment and condemnation, like a lot of Christians he knew. I wanted the best for him and was willing to let him see my spiritual shortcomings. Before long, Street became a Christian himself.

The more time Street and I spent together, the more we talked about collaborating on something in the studio. He knew I felt called to produce music for more than just Christians, and one day he had a crazy idea: I should make a mixtape . . . and give it away for free.

171

Street believed that many people could benefit from the music but would never come into contact with it in our current model. My music was only known among Christians. Street said that a Christian artist can't just put out an album and expect non-Christians to buy it. He wanted to take the route that the broader rap community takes when trying to gain exposure. Drop a mixtape. Give it away for free. Allow people to taste and see what we were doing. This was our best chance to get the music poppin' in the streets.

The idea made me nervous. I didn't know how people would respond, but it felt authentic to who I was. Street had a relationship with one of the biggest DJs in hip-hop, DJ Don Cannon, who was eager to join us and host the project. The next step was to actually write it.

172

I sat down, took a deep breath, and let the music flow out of me. I could see the faces of the people I was writing to in my mind. They looked different than before. I was no longer envisioning the megachurch pastors I wanted to accept me, and I wasn't picturing the fans who would look up to me because I had "figured it all out." Now I was seeing people like me and Street. People who grew up in the hood, who faced serious problems at too young an age. People who were surrounded by all sorts of sin. People who needed hope and encouragement and truth and the gospel.

I STARTED TALKING *TO* PEOPLE INSTEAD OF *AT* PEOPLE.

I started talking *to* people instead of *at* people. The result was a mixtape we called "Church Clothes." The lyrics were stripped of most of the Christian-ese that shackled my previous music, even *Rehab*. Rather than try to preach at people, the songs dealt with real problems head-on. In "Cold World," I talked about the difficulties of living in a broken world of poverty and violence. One song, "The Price of Life," dealt with rampant materialism:

> *She camouflage her insecurity in Jimmy Choos*
> *High heels but the mountain top she'll never choose*
> *She'll settle for a dude in precious metals*
> *A slave to his money; by his chains you can tell it*

Church Clothes was more than just an honest album. In some ways the album was the definitive declaration of my new direction. I was proclaiming that the music I was committed to making was for all people. I was declaring that I was no longer striving to be Christianity's golden child or get a pat on the back from religious celebrities. I was going to have the conversations I felt God calling me to curate. I was going to tell real and raw stories and let the chips fall where they may.

In this way, *Church Clothes* was a manifesto of who I felt God had called me to be: a hip-hop artist who is a Christian, but doesn't fit inside a box. I had always been a truth-teller, but now I was speaking in a way that made sense to people outside of the Christian faith, too. The title track was even written from the perspective of a non-Christian. It talked about hypocrisy and corrupt pastors and gay choir members who are stuck in the closet.

The honesty resonated, and the mixtape blew up on DatPiff. It was downloaded more than 100,000 times in the first forty-eight hours. The traffic overloaded their servers and crashed the website. A quarter of a million people snatched it up by the end of the month. We were all shocked.

But while the music was surging, some of my Christian fans were confused by the new direction. Looking back, I should have been more explicit with what God was leading me to do. My silence left my longtime fans in the dark about the evolution of the music. The dam of their frustration broke less than a year later when I released my next studio album, *Gravity*, which pushed even further. I even teamed up with mainstream rapper Big K.R.I.T. on one of the tracks. Some thought I had gone too far.

Former fans wrote hateful things about me on blogs. They labeled me a "sellout" and a "fake." Some attacked me personally, even questioning whether I was really a Christian. Some people contacted venues and tours to get me banned from performing. Crowds started showing up to protest my concerts. People were posting YouTube videos condemning me to hell, and even suggesting I had joined the Illuminati.

I was being criticized in public for the first time in my career, and I didn't know how to manage it. I was angry and hurt at first. I protested in prayer: "If these are your people, God, I don't want to be like them!" I even flipped out to my wife, screaming about how betrayed I felt. I was just trying to follow God's calling on my life, I told her. I was still unashamed of my faith—that hadn't changed— but now I was being bold with my art. Why were people attacking me?

My wise wife encouraged me to get off social media and spend some time with God. I knew she was right. I grabbed a few books, my Bible, and locked myself in my closet. I read a biography of Francis Schaeffer, a Christian thinker who showed the world what it meant to live with a Christian worldview. Schaeffer knew what being criticized felt like, and it drove him to make sure he knew what he believed too.

Reading Schaeffer sent me back, once again, to the Gospels. I read about how Jesus' heart for the world incited the anger of the religious community. But it never stopped Him from doing what He believed the Father was calling Him to do, even if that meant laying His livelihood and His life on the altar. If religious people wanted to crucify me for trying to reach the non-religious, I concluded, I was in pretty good company.

I emerged from my closet with a new confidence and peace. And a few days later I had a conversation with pastor Rick Warren that confirmed everything God had been saying.

"If you're going to call the shots, Lecrae, you're going to have to take them too," he told me. "For every one thousand people you influence, you'll have one hundred critics. And many of them will call themselves Christian. That just comes with the territory."

Once again, I committed to die to the acceptance of men. To refocus all my attention on God's glory and His calling on my life. I had learned to be unashamed in the midst of a *fallen* world. Now I needed to learn to be unashamed in the midst of a *religious* world.

> I HAD LEARNED TO BE UNASHAMED IN THE MIDST OF A *FALLEN* WORLD. NOW I NEEDED TO LEARN TO BE UNASHAMED IN THE MIDST OF A *RELIGIOUS* WORLD.

I started to realize that Christian bloggers and critics will find a reason to scrutinize almost anything. At my first mainstream hip-hop festival—Paid Dues Festival in Los Angeles—I performed after Macklemore. At another festival, I performed alongside Wu-Tang Clan. People went out of their way to express frustrations at me sharing a stage with these "secular artists." Some critics were angry that a YouTube video showed me rocking my head to "profane music." But my critics almost lost their minds when they became aware of my friendship with Kendrick Lamar.

But the critics didn't know the whole story. Critics almost never do.

They claimed I had been seduced by the money. They didn't know that I was actually *losing* money at many of these mainstream events. The Christian world paid better and treated me like royalty. But I was paying out of my pocket to fly my crew out to some of these festivals because I was serious about being salt and light in these places.

The critics said I was just chasing fame by trying to become friends with famous people. But they didn't know that I was an outsider at many of these events. I wasn't sacrificing my beliefs or seeking their acceptance. I wasn't smoking weed or going to the strip clubs with everyone else.

The critics claimed I was a sell-out for being friends with people like Kendrick. They were mad that I didn't call him out for the profanity in his music. They didn't know that he and I were constantly dialoguing about faith. The critics hated that I was loving this community instead of attacking them. They didn't know that rappers would often come find me after a show—sometimes high and out of their minds—and ask me to help figure out what God wanted for their lives.

Critics always have a lot of fury. But they rarely have a lot of facts.

By God's grace, the music was resonating with many despite the frustration of a few. Our mainstream fan base was growing. And many of the Christians who were initially confused by the new direction were starting to come around too. For everyone we lost, we gained ten more. The question now was not whether the fans could handle the music, but whether I could handle my newfound success and all its temptations.

> **CRITICS ALWAYS HAVE A LOT OF FURY. BUT THEY RARELY HAVE A LOT OF FACTS.**

11 -
THE
OUTSIDERS

———

We are the odd,

The outcast,

The peculiar,

The strangers.

And they say we don't fit in

But I say, we are exactly who God created us to be: anomalies

The system didn't plan for this.

Lecrae | "Anomaly" | *Anomaly*

———

A dozen bulbs shine from around the border of the mirror. The light illuminates my face, allowing me to stare back at my reflection. The voices of a dozen friends standing behind me have faded. The room is silent as far as I am concerned. They say if you can make it in New York, you can make it anywhere. I'm about to find out if that old saying is true. It is April 9, 2015, and I'm sitting in a backstage dressing room in the heart of Times Square.

People lined up hours earlier to get into the Best Buy Theater for the sold-out show tonight. A reporter with the *New York Times* is here to see the show for a story he's writing. Earlier in the day, I performed live on *Good Morning America*. Days before that, my music video premiered at halftime at a Brooklyn Nets game.

These great opportunities are also incredible temptations.

Two thousand years ago, the apostle John wrote, "For all that is in the world—the desires of the flesh and the desires of the eyes and pride of life—is not from the Father but is from the world."[17] Not much has changed in two millennia. Achieving what the world calls "success" has taught me that these are still three of the world's main temptations.

The desires of the flesh are the physical pleasures that fallen humans crave. Namely, lust and sex. Early in my career, women were very respectful. Because they respected what I was about and what I stood for. But as the music became more mainstream, I attracted fans who just liked the sound of the music, rather than its message. So female fans got more flirtatious.

On tour, beautiful women would walk past me, wink, and then slip their phone number into my pocket. On social media, fans would tweet that I'm the man of their dreams and they will "do anything" to be with me. But the ones who are slick and sly about it are the most dangerous. Women would come up and try to connect with me "professionally." Some would just hand me their card and ask me to call them for a business opportunity. I could usually tell the vibe was off.

I learned quickly to set up safeguards against the desires of my flesh. When women hand me a card, I pass it to my manager. When women hand me a phone number, I immediately give them to the guys who look out for me on the road, and they shred them.

The desires of the eyes are a craving for everything we see. It is the desire for "stuff." When you're in the entertainment industry, you're surrounded by the finer things of life. People pick you up in $300,000 Bentley convertibles and invite you to sail on their yachts. There is always a glamorous party happening somewhere, and each seems to be more over-the-top than the last.

I grew accustomed to these things over time, even though I knew I didn't need them. I was traveling all the time and always getting upgraded on flights. When I didn't, I would wrestle internally. I'd do a few performances in a row where they'd put me up at expensive hotels. And then I'd struggle to be appreciative when another event put me in a two-star hotel. When we'd perform at theme parks, I'd be escorted to the front of the lines. And then I'd have to work to be patient when I had to wait to ride a roller coaster.

You know your heart is in trouble when luxuries become expectations. Early on, I had to repent of the way I was falling to this temptation. I knew if I followed this path, it would warp me. I started doing music to serve people, not to have people serve me. I wanted the music to produce transformed lives, not trophies. As the music spread, I prayed more often that God would keep me humble and true to my calling. What does it profit a rapper to gain the whole world and lose his soul?

The decisions I've made in my *personal* life have helped me resist the temptations I face in my *professional* life. I was lucky early in my career and was given wise counsel to cap my salary and live below my means. Money itself isn't evil, but the love of it is the root of all kinds of evil. So these things helped me to stay grounded. I began realizing that people on yachts weren't happier than people in rowboats. Bentleys break down just like Nissans. You can get a great night's sleep at a Hampton Inn just like at a Ritz-Carlton. And flying in first class won't get you to your destination any faster than riding in coach.

WHAT DOES IT PROFIT A RAPPER TO GAIN THE WHOLE WORLD AND LOSE HIS SOUL?

Actually, the "lesser" things in life often end up being the better things in life. Because they build character. Those with character are usually those who leave a lasting mark on the world. And whoever dies with the most stuff, still dies. So it is an empty ambition. As I wrote in "Confe$$ions":

> *I've flown first class, flown private jets*
> *Rode in the foreign cars, still so unimpressed . . .*
> *But if you find identity in it then go and forget it*
> *You gain the whole world but lost the only thing ya' own*
> *'Cause everything else is just a temporary loan*

John's third temptation, the pride of life, is the desire to root our identity in achievement. The real problem with success is not that you are accomplishing great things; it's that people are constantly telling you how great you are. "You deserve more," they say. Or, "With your talent, you should be paid better." Or, "You're better than this, Lecrae."

Because of my background, success is a deadly viper that should be handled with care. I still battle the desire for acceptance. Sometimes every day. There can be ten thousand adoring fans at my show, but the two people who trashed me online will often dominate my thoughts. I've forgotten that the two don't matter. And neither do the ten thousand. It only matters what the One thinks.

My desire for acceptance is one of the crosses that I carry. Each morning I have to attend a funeral. My own. I have to wake up and once again die to my desires for people's approval.

183

Competition is at the heart of the pride of life. But as a follower of Jesus, I have to remember that success is not what I've done compared with what others have done. Success is what I've done compared with what God has called me to do. By learning to exist *in* culture while resisting the temptations *of* culture, I was forced to face a different type of temptation: the pressure to conform.

> **EACH MORNING I HAVE TO ATTEND A FUNERAL. MY OWN.**

★ ★ ★

In the months leading up to my performance in Times Square, the music penetrated the mainstream masses like never before. *Rehab* broke into the top 20 on the Billboard top 200 charts and earned a Grammy nomination. *Gravity* charted at #3 on Billboard and actually won a Grammy. But my latest album, *Anomaly*, debuted at #1 on the Billboard 200 and won a Grammy after being nominated for three.

This catapulted me into a new arena where I was being profiled by *Time* and *XXL* and being invited to perform on big stages at places like South by Southwest. But mainstream success brought a new set of challenges with it. Popular musicians come into contact with all kinds of people. Some of them just want to use you. They make empty promises, trying to earn your trust so they can ride your wave. Others genuinely respect you, but the first type of person makes you skeptical.

I wasn't sure who to trust or how to proceed. It was like leaving training camp and walking straight onto the football field and having someone hand me a ball while fifty thousand screaming fans wait to see which play I was going to run. There was pressure to become the person the mainstream wanted me to be. In a situation like this, you can expect the player to make some mistakes. And I made plenty.

One of my biggest problems was that I didn't know how to navigate mainstream media interviews with big-time music outlets like BET, MTV, and *Billboard*. When people viewed or read my comments, they assumed I was just speaking from my heart. But my guard wasn't down; it was higher than ever. I'd be standing in front of journalists with adrenaline pumping through my veins and praying that I didn't mess up. It's not easy. They ask a tough question, and I'm trying to formulate a perfect answer on the spot. I remember one interview I did with Hard Knock TV where I dropped the ball. I stumbled over my answers and didn't really articulate what I believed. The interview was parsed by Christian critics who accused me of becoming "worldly." But I was just nervous.

So mainstream forces were pushing me to conform to their expectations, and Christian critics were trying to pull me into their camp. I had to finally accept that there just wasn't a category for what God was calling me to do. I wasn't making Gospel music or Christian music. But it contrasted with the majority of mainstream music as well. In a twist of irony, I realized I had become what I had always been.

An outsider . . .

A misfit . . .

An anomaly . . .

I had the title for my next album.

The record represented the final stage of my evolution as an artist. I was no longer trying to fit into the boxes— the prisons—that other artists lived in. I wasn't working to impress the gatekeepers and kingmakers in the Christian or mainstream worlds. They both were building lesser kingdoms, and I was going to seek a greater one—God's kingdom.

The *Anomaly* album was almost completely autobiographical. It walked people through the story God had written through my life since birth, and the place He had finally brought me to. The opening track, "Outsiders," summed it all up:

Now I realize that I'm free
And I realize that I'm me
And I found out that I'm not alone 'cause there's plenty
*   people like me*
That's right, there's plenty people like me
All love me, despite me
And all unashamed and all unafraid to speak out for
*   what we might see*

I felt liberated as I waited to perform at the Best Buy Theater that night. The long journey that led me to this moment was covered in God's fingerprints. It's easy, of course, to recognize God's presence in the good times— my conversion night in Atlanta, meeting my wife, launching Reach Records, and the ongoing success of the music. But I now realized God had been there on the darkest nights of my life too.

God didn't walk out the door when my dad did.

As a child in Southeast San Diego struggling to fit in, God showed up in Big Momma's prayers and Brother Santiago's sermons.

During my identity crisis at college and while I sat outside the women's clinic, God was waiting for me to come to my senses.

As I lay sleeping after trying to overdose on pills, God stood watch.

When I checked into rehab, God revealed Himself through Bible pages and crayon scribblings.

He came to me through the words of James White and Charles Spurgeon and Frederick Douglass and Nancy Pearcey and Andy Crouch.

When the critics' words cut deep, God showed up in the wisdom of my wife and the kind words of a pastor-friend.

Someone told me recently that people are like tree trunks. They have many rings inside that mark what they once were. Staring into the mirror backstage at that Manhattan theater, I asked the question that had been plaguing me since my birth: "Who is Lecrae? Who is he *really*?"

Was I the rebel kid? The lost college student who just wanted to be accepted? The legalistic man who battled self-righteousness? Was I a husband or a father or a hip-hop artist? Like a tree trunk, all those people were a part of me. They *are* a part of me. But more than anything, Lecrae is a child who is unconditionally loved by God. I'm a sinner who has been rescued by God from my brokenness and called to glorify the One who has never left my side.

187

That's who Lecrae is, and that's who I'll always be.

Before I took the stage, there was only one thing left to do. I gathered up our team to pray like we always do before performing:

> *Father, allow us to use our gifts to paint an accurate picture of Your creativity and your goodness tonight. Help us to stay out of the way of Your will being done. We want to play a role, but we don't want to take the lead. We are extras in Your movie, but not the star of this show.*
>
> *May we be humble.*
>
> *May we be grateful.*
>
> *May we be unashamed.*
>
> *Amen.*

+ –

GOD'S
POETRY

———

I used to wonder what I would live for
'Til I found what I would die for
Found the reason I'm alive for
I'm only here to help the people turn they lights on

Lecrae | "Illuminate"

———

"You can't listen to the radio, Lecrae," he said. "You're a Christian."

Those were the words of a twelve-year-old named Dante that I mentored in Binghampton. I had given him some of my music, and it was his first serious introduction to God and Jesus and faith. One day I picked him up, and when he jumped in my car, Young Jeezy was playing on the radio. His head snapped to the side, and that's when he told me I wasn't supposed to listen to "secular" music.

I asked him what he was talking about, and he explained that Christians had to stop listening to "worldly music." He said that Christians should only listen to "Christian music." He could listen to secular stuff because he wasn't a Christian, but I shouldn't. We kept talking, and he told me that he thought Christians had to follow a list of dos and don'ts to keep God from getting mad.

"Wait," I interrupted, "you believe that in order for God to love you, you have to stop doing certain things and start doing other things?"

His view of Christianity was mainly coming from me and my music. Somehow he had gotten the idea that following Jesus was all about what he did, not who he trusted. He assumed that "Christian" music was just for Christians and "secular" music was just for non-Christians. In his mind, the two genres and audiences should remain separate. I've never forgotten that conversation, and it was one of the catalysts for rethinking the music.

Most of the non-Christians and many of the Christians I know see the world like Dante did. Like I once did. They think they view the world through a single lens, but really they are looking through bifocals. Half the world is sacred, holy, or good, and half the world is secular, unholy, or evil. But when we see the world through a divided lens, we can easily end up living divided lives. We act one way in church or any other "sacred" space. Then we act another way when we're out with our friends in "secular" spaces. And the result is that the things of God rarely come into contact with or influence the world.

The solution to this problem is to begin to develop a biblical worldview. While nearly 80 percent of all Americans claim to be Christian, only 9 percent have a biblical worldview.[18] If you are a follower of Jesus, this should frighten you. Because more than likely, you're in the majority and probably don't even realize it.

So what is a biblical worldview, and how should it change the way we live?

A biblical worldview is, by definition, rooted in Scripture. So we begin at the beginning. The first chapter of the book of Genesis. It is a familiar story of a God that creates, of a serpent that tempts, and of two humans who commit the first sin. Here we find the basic elements of a biblical worldview:

1. *God creates all things.* So we know there is a single, sovereign, transcendent, all-powerful God who is creative and artistic. Because He declares His creation "good," we know that matter matters. The physical world is not just an intermediate place where we exist until we die and go somewhere.

191

2. *God creates humans in His image.* This means that every person is uniquely valuable. They are not just objects to be used for pleasure or progress. Every person is the object of God's love; and therefore, they should be treated with dignity and respect.

3. *Despite having God's image, the first humans disobeyed God.* The story of Adam and Eve eating the forbidden fruit is my story and your story too. We all reject God's rightful rule over the world, disobeying His wishes for our lives. Sin leads to brokenness between humans and God, each other, and themselves. If you want to know what is wrong with the world, the answer is always sin.

4. *God promises that one day the serpent that tempted Adam and Eve will be crushed.* This reminds us that while we should not minimize or ignore sin, we do not live in

despair. We have hope. God has not abandoned His creation. He sent Christ to crush the serpent. When Jesus lives in us, we have the same power to stomp out the sin that the serpent has brought into the world.

These elements remind us that the world God created is "good." Things aren't inherently evil or bad. But they have been tainted with sin. Because of Jesus, we don't need to see culture as something to be avoided. It is something to be engaged. You cannot stomp something you're running away from. You can't influence something you never encounter.

A good example of a biblical worldview is Daniel. I like Daniel. If he were alive now, we'd probably hang out. In the Bible, Daniel was an advisor to a king named Nebuchadnezzar. Working for the king was a pretty good gig, but things got weird when the king had some crazy dreams. Nebuchadnezzar wanted to know what they meant, so he summoned his advisors. In those days, interpreting dreams was a pagan practice. If Daniel was wearing bifocals, he would have seen this as a secular action. An evil action. Something that people who serve God didn't do.

But Daniel didn't see the world like that. He knew that, as the Psalmist would later write, "The earth is the LORD's, and everything in it."[19] So Daniel went to God, and God told him what the dreams meant. When Daniel interpreted King Nebuchanezzar's dreams, the king was impressed and appointed Daniel his chief advisor.

Now if Daniel were living in our world, he might have turned down the job and enrolled in seminary. But he didn't. Because he saw this "secular" job as part of his "sacred" calling. And because he didn't see the world as divided, he took the job and was able to speak godly wisdom into Nebuchadnezzar's life.

This has changed the way I do music. There is no such thing as Christian rap and secular rap. Only people can become Christians. Music can't accept Jesus into its heart. So I am not trying to make Christian music or secular music. I'm just making music. Hip-hop, like all music, is a good thing. I could use it for evil by filling it with violence and misogyny and profanity. Or I can use it to glorify God. Every song I write doesn't have to have the Gospel spelled out or quote Scripture so that people will know I love Jesus. My goal is just to use my gifts to produce great art that tells the truth about the world. If I see the world through a biblical lens, the music will naturally paint a picture that serves people and honors God.

The same is true for you. If you are a politician, you don't have a "secular" job. If you are a computer programmer, you don't have a "secular" job. The term *secular* is defined as an attitude, activity, or thing that has no religious or spiritual basis. But there is *nothing* on the planet that God isn't ruling over. Everything a believer touches and uses in a way that honors God is, in a sense, no longer "secular." We all bring our sacred callings into a world that God created and called "good" and that has been tainted by sin, but where God wants to use us to impact for His glory.

What is true for a job is true for everything in the world that God has called "good." Dancing is good, movies are good, music is good. The hearts of men, however, have been tainted by sin. So the way we use these good things can be bad. Some Christians have talked about sex like it is inherently bad. You can use it for evil by becoming a prostitute, but you can also use it for good by enjoying the gift of sex in the context of marriage. If I stab you with a knife, that's evil. But I can also use that knife to carve a Thanksgiving turkey for a family in need.

Rather than thinking about the world in the categories of simply good and evil, a biblical worldview helps us think in the categories of good and redeemable. You and I may come from different backgrounds and live in different cities and have different jobs and be separated in age by decades, but we have the same calling: to be instruments of God's redemptive power in the world.

> YOU AND I MAY COME FROM DIFFERENT BACKGROUNDS AND LIVE IN DIFFERENT CITIES AND HAVE DIFFERENT JOBS AND BE SEPARATED IN AGE BY DECADES, BUT WE HAVE THE SAME CALLING: TO BE INSTRUMENTS OF GOD'S REDEMPTIVE POWER IN THE WORLD.

The apostle Paul wrote, "We are his workmanship, created in Christ Jesus for good works, which God prepared beforehand, that we should walk in them."[20] The word for workmanship is *poema*. We are God's poem to the world.

A poem articulates the heart, the mind, and the character of the poet. Your calling may not be to write music or produce music or sing music, but that's okay. You *are* music. You're God's music. And God doesn't just want to break records and top charts with you; He wants to change lives and industries and society.

By God's grace, I'm going to keep making the music as long as I have air in my lungs. But my prayer is that you'll make music too. Maybe not with your voice, and maybe not on a stage, but hopefully with your life. And may God get glory from the music we create.

Keep on creating,

> MY PRAYER IS THAT YOU'LL MAKE MUSIC TOO. MAYBE NOT WITH YOUR VOICE, AND MAYBE NOT ON A STAGE, BUT HOPEFULLY WITH YOUR LIFE.

ACKNOWLEDGMENTS

I don't even know how to begin to thank the many people who have played a role in both my life and the completion of this book.

There is my wonderful wife who has stood by me in a million storms and my kids who are a part of a new legacy and new normal. Thank you for all the late nights and days away.

My grandmother, who sowed the first seeds of faith into my little heart: Your example is everything to me. My mother who pushed me beyond what I thought I could be and made me resilient and tough. My stepdad, who did the best he knew how and has become a voice in my world helping me navigate and think responsibly. My sisters and brothers for supporting me and not disowning me! My uncles and aunts for helping raise me. My Uncle Chris, I love and admire you. You were barely twenty but you were my hero. You didn't ask for that kind of responsibility; and even if you didn't know what you were doing, I know you loved me. Thank you Pops and Granna Kemp. You adopted me as the son you never had and I'm forever grateful. See you on the other side Pops.

The Kemp family, y'all have supported me from day one. Y'all are not my in-laws; y'all are just family!

James White: Thank you for your faithfulness. Your preaching and teaching have walked me from dark to light. Thank you for being there for some of the most important parts of my life. Ben Washer: There are not enough words to describe how divine your role in my life is. Your self-lessness has fueled my dreams and passions. BJ, AT, Tedashii, Nate R., Keynon, Josh R., and Adam Donyes: Thank you for your REAL no-holds-barred, no judgment, no excuses friendship. I'm better because of you men. Trip, Andy, KB, Sho Baraka: Thanks for challenging me and being there.

Soup and Linda Campbell: You changed mine and my wife, Darragh's lives. Thank you for being the leaders we needed and helping us grow up. Dhati Lewis, man you started this mess! You always believed in us more than we believed in ourselves. I still look up to you! James and Tarsh: Lord KNOWS we wouldn't be here without you. Our sanity, sanctification, and sobriety is due to your love and godliness. Miguel and DA: Thanks so much for your friendship!

198

My H-town Family, my Dallas Family, my Denver Family, my Cali Family: THANK YOU! I'm who I am because of you! Cross Movement, IMPACT, Plumbline, UNT, KAA, Kanankuk, Fellowship Memphis, Blueprint Church, Cornerstone, Denton Bible, The Village Church, Oak Cliff Bible Fellowship, Epiphany Fellowship, and the countless others who have supported me through the years: Thank you. Thank you Renovation Church and Pastor Léonce for supporting and shepherding my soul.

40 Deep Management: Thanks for the tireless hours of work. My road crew: I love y'all. All the artists and

producers: Thanks for your love! Yates & Yates: Thank you for sowing this seed of writing in the first place. I wouldn't be writing were it not for you. Jonathan Merritt: Friend, there are literally no words to describe how humbled and grateful I am for you. You have helped me walk into a new season. B&H: Your faith in the work God is doing in me and the support you have shown is mind-blowing. Thank you for partnering with me to be a light in a dark world. Bryan, you are the eyes and ears of my whole operation! Without you, I crumble! Reach Family! You are priceless gems. You are the blood in the veins of our impact. I can't thank you enough. Keep scrumming for change!

To all the 116 Unashamed family all over the world: I couldn't do it without you. We are a movement!

I'm sure I forgot someone. Please forgive me! It proves how imperfect I am and how gracious you are!

ABOUT LECRAE

Lecrae is a two-time Grammy Award-winning hip-hop artist whose studio albums and mixtapes have sold nearly two million copies. His 2014 album, *Anomaly*, debuted at #1 on the Billboard 200, Rap, Digital, Christian, Gospel, and Independent charts. That same year, Lecrae co-headlined the highest-selling tour in America, beating out Beyonce, Justin Timberlake, and Elton John. He has been nominated for five Grammy Awards, fourteen Dove Awards, a Billboard Music Award, a Soul Train Award, and a BET Hip Hop Award.

In addition to earning accolades for his musical talent, Lecrae has gained wide recognition for maintaining a strong commitment to his faith and values. Remaining true to his beliefs has made Lecrae into an artist that redefines mainstream popular culture.

He is founder of ReachLife Ministries, a non-profit that seeks to bridge the gap between faith and the urban context. In 2013, he partnered with NBA player Dwayne Wade and former Obama White House staffer Joshua Dubois to launch a national initiative "devoted to restoring America's commitment to fatherhood." He was also named NFL Player's Choice Performer during the 2013 Super Bowl in recognition of his positive lyrics.

Lecrae resides in Atlanta, Georgia, with his wife, Darragh, and three children.

Twitter: @Lecrae
Instagram: @Lecrae
Facebook: www.facebook.com/Lecrae

NOTES

1. Mychal Denzel Smith, "Hip-Hop Father Figures?", *The Root*, June 30, 2011, http://www.theroot.com /articles/culture/2011/06/hiphop_father_figures. html.
2. Proverbs 12:18 NIV.
3. ABC 10, "Guns and Drugs Seized, 93 Arrested in 'Operation Red Sky,'" http://www.10news. com/news/guns-and-drugs-seized-93-arrested- in-operation-red-sky.
4. NKJV.
5. James 1:8 KJV.
6. Rom. 1:6 NASB.
7. Rom. 1:22 NASB.
8. Rom. 1:21 NASB.
9. Rom. 2:8–9 NASB.
10. Rom. 6:21–23 NASB.
11. Rom. 1:16 NASB.
12. This is an old saying attributed to Martin Luther.
13. Nancy Pearcey, *Total Truth: Liberating Christianity from Its Cultural Captivity* (Wheaton, IL: Crossway, 2005).
14. Andy Crouch, *Culture Making: Recovering Our Creative Calling* (Downers Grove, IL: InterVarsity, 2008).
15. Matthew 16:16 ESV.
16. Matthew 16:17–18 ESV.
17. 1 John 2:16 ESV.

18. See http://www.pewforum.org/2015/05/12/
americas-changing-religious-landscape; https://
barna.org/barna-update/transformation/252-
barna-survey-examines-changes-in-worldview-
among-christians-over-the-past-13-years#.
Vm44Xr-K0ro.

19. Psalm 24:1 ESV.

20. Ephesians 2:10 ESV.

206

208

209

211